MW00748480

Break Time at Ernie's

Photography and text by

KEVIN ADAMS

Special thanks to Daren Schmaltz
for the archived Dwarf car photos.

DWARF CAR INDUSTRIES

Break Time at Ernie's by Kevin Adams

© 2017 Kevin Adams

All rights reserved. No portion of this book may be reproduced in any form without permission from the publisher, except as permitted by U.S. copyright law.

Published by Dwarf Car Industries LLC
53443 W. Century Rd.
Maricopa, AZ 85139

www.DwarfCarPromotions.com

The Dwarf Car Industries logo is a trademark of Dwarf Car Industries LLC.
For permissions contact: dwarfcarpromotions@gmail.com

This book is typeset in Avenir typeface family.

ISBN: 978-1-5323-5368-0
First Edition.

Book & Cover Design by Igor Brezhnev (www.igorbrezhnev.com)
Creative & Print Direction by Joey Robert Parks (www.joeyrobertparks.com)

I DECIDED MY FATHER'S STORY NEEDED TO BE TOLD

It was spring, 2011. I packed a cooler with cold drinks and headed over to 4:30 break time at Ernie Adams Dwarf car shop. As I slid open the large steel doors to Ernie's shop, he stopped working and asked, "Break time?" Ernie will always take the first five minutes to show you his work for the day. I have seen my father's work since I was a child and, to this day, I'm absolutely amazed what he can do with a flat piece of steel. As I pulled the top of my beer can open, Ernie handed me two thank you letters from a local car show he had recently attended. The letters were only two of many others he had received. It was at this time that I decided people need to see Ernie's remarkable talent and the extremely detailed craftsmanship that he puts into each individual part, adding up to a true work of art, second to none.

Kris Adams

CONTENTS

Chapter 1

A Look Through The Window

IT WAS 1944 WHEN LITTLE ERNIE ADAMS AND HIS FAMILY ROLLED INTO THE SMALL TOWN OF HARVARD, NEBRASKA. Down Main Street and across the railroad tracks, they drove in a 1929 Chevy navigated by Ernie's father. Behind it, he pulled another '29 Chevy guided by Ernie's mom, along with several goats as passengers.

Left: **Ernie's first Dwarf car in an early stage. This car was originally built as a touring car with an 18-hp Wisconsin motor and solid-rubber tires on aluminum wheels. He used a homemade hacksaw made from a chair frame, hammer and chisel to build the body.**

Right: **Ernie and his middle son, Kevin, in 1973 before the top was added.**

"I remember the story my parents told me of how the townspeople laughed as we drove through town," recalled Ernie. South of the tracks and a half-mile east, his family settled on three acres purchased at the right price of $150. Their first home was a 28'-homemade trailer. "We called it The Car House," said Ernie. "My father worked to fix up an old, two-room house on our land that we later move into."

From his earliest memories, Ernie had an incredible fascination for cars and engines. "When I was in school, I liked to build small cars," he said. He built carts of all kinds to push or tow. If he could put wheels on it he did. As he got older, he attached engines to bicycles, tricycles and tools that were originally hand-cranked. He actually made one of the first gas-powered wicker wheelchairs. He proudly entered it in the town parade and rode it right up Main Street.

When asked where he got the idea for building a Dwarf car Ernie answered, "When I was 15, I was sitting at our kitchen table. I looked through the window and saw a tire swing lying up against the body of an old refrigerator. It looked like a touring car with a black fender. I knew from that moment, I wanted to build a car like that."

Ernie's vision of that tire swing lying against the old refrigerator remained in his memory until 1962, when he married his wife, Sheila. He settled down with his new bride and found himself with a lot of spare time. He was able to get his hands on an old refrigerator and began to build a car body as he remembered back in his youth. He used parts from eight other refrigerators and cut them with a homemade saw he built from an old chair frame. His vision of a homemade touring car became a reality, and the first Dwarf car was born.

In the early 1980's Ernie added a top, 12" pneumatic tires, and a 2-cylinder 13-hp Onan motor. The car now weighed around 900 lbs. and had features such as bucket seats, cloth interior, operational windows, and a vinyl top. Because this is the first Dwarf car ever built, it is known as the 'Grandpa Dwarf.' This car is kept in running order and is still driven today.

Ernie began drawing cars as early as kindergarten.
At age 5, Ernie sketched this drawing as a school assignment.
He continued to draw car pictures throughout
his school days, and his creativity grew as he did.

Ernie's drawing of a 1930 Ford sedan at age 14

Ernie's drawing of a 1930 Ford coupe at age 14

At the age of 10, Ernie mounted a 4-stroke washing machine engine to his pedal bicycle.

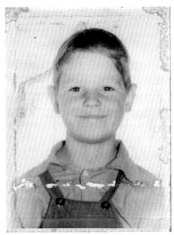

Age 7 **Age 15** **Age 21**

Soon after Ernie built his little car, he found a passion for racing cars. It was 1965 in Council Bluffs, Iowa when Ernie and a buddy attended the Saturday night stock car races at Playland Speedway. Right away, Ernie knew he wanted to race! After finding a 1955 Ford junker, he built a 352 motor to power the car. With light-green paint color, white wheels, and the number 24, he was ready for the local quarter-mile asphalt circle track.

It wasn't long before he wanted more power. After hopping up the 352 motor Ernie wanted to race the half-mile dirt oval at Whitehead Speedway in Nebraska City, Nebraska. The old Ford ran great on the dirt. With a seventh-place car, Ernie managed to end up around third place each race.

In 1968, Ernie narrowly escaped death. In turn four, his car began rolling end over end down the straightaway and around turn one before stopping short of turn two. The ride of Ernie's life miraculously left him with only a few bruises and eyes like two black olives. The car was completely totaled. He had a twin to his car at home, one he raced the year before, and the following weekend he amazed the crowd by having his car repaired and ready to race after such a horrific crash.

After Ernie's crash, a man by the name of Ron Bockert approached him. "I like the way you drive and I'd like to see your Ford beat the Chevrolets," said Ron. The two became partners and agreed Ernie would remain the driver. After a rough season of blowing motors, their Ford burned up the track the following season. In a 1962 Ford with a 406 motor, Ernie won every heat race, every trophy dash, and every main event he drove in that year. He was awarded the championship in the Late Model Stock Car Division in 1971 at Whitehead Speedway.

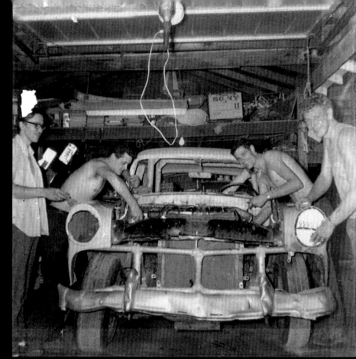

In the spring of 2011, I decided my father's story needed to be told. My name is Kevin, Ernie's middle son. I grew up on the south side of Phoenix, Arizona with my dad, mom and two brothers. It was fall of 1971 when my father moved our family west from Council Bluffs, Iowa, to escape the bitter-cold winters. Ernie had purchased a new mobile home in 1969 and decided he would move it to Phoenix. After pricing the move, he found he could buy his own truck and relocate the mobile home himself. He found a used 1963 International mobile home toter, put on a new paint job, and was on his way to new adventures.

Ernie was ready for a new start once in Phoenix. He held onto his homemade little car but decided his stock car racing days were over. A beautiful yard with big trees and a nice, green lawn is what Ernie wanted now. With all this in mind, he positioned his home for a very small backyard and an extra-large yard in front. Right away, Ernie planted several large trees, dug a fishpond, and began watching the grass grow.

It wasn't long before the fire inside Ernie began to burn again. His passion for engines and cars was still there; he had a dilemma now. He didn't leave any space in his backyard to build a shop. A 20' x 12' area at the rear of his house is all he had to work with. Using a wheelbarrow, he and a friend mixed up and laid a modest concrete pad. Ernie revamped a steel garden shed he bought and put it on the new cement pad, then used a wood foundation to raise the shed one foot and added custom, double-swinging doors. Next, he began to fill the new shop with tools, most of which came from the local swap meet or anywhere he could get a deal. The incredible work he would do in this little shop would someday change the automobile world.

One of Ernie's first projects was building a two-passenger bicycle-car for my brothers and me. I remember my dad driving us over to the city dump where we loaded up every bicycle frame, wheel and handlebar we could find. The car sported four wheels, a full steering assembly along with a steering wheel, and two sets of chain-driven pedals. Both the driver and passenger powered the car. I remember spending equal time patching inner tubes as time spent driving the car.

Our neighborhood was in a rural desert area at the foot of a large mountain range. Ernie bought a dirt bike motorcycle to climb the rugged mountains with. He met a few friends with the same interest in climbing the mountains. There was a young man named Daren Schmaltz that Ernie became good friends with. Daren decided to build a new hill-climbing machine.

Ernie moved his 12' x 60' mobile home 1,500 miles from Council Bluffs, Iowa to Phoenix, Arizona in 1971. This was Ernie's first truck-driving experience. You might say he had 'on-the-job training.'

Ernie's three sons Rick, Kevin and Jason enjoy the two-passenger bicycle-car Ernie made for them in 1975.

Using his Volkswagen Karmann Ghia, Daren built a homemade dune buggy that would crawl right up the rough mountains. After seeing Daren's buggy go, Ernie said to himself, "I've got to have one." He began thinking outside the box of what a typical dune buggy would look like. Ernie had an old Ford straight-6 motor he could use for a power plant. Instead of a typical rear-mounted engine, Ernie positioned the motor in the front. He also used a Ford transmission and 9" rear end. Four donated orange kitchen chairs with the legs cut off were used for seating. He was not a man of money but he was resourceful in using what was available.

After a few wheel-standing trial runs in Ernie's new dune buggy, it was apparent there was not enough weight in the front end and the suspension was too stiff. This only made the ride more exciting, driving up steep mountains on two wheels. In some instances, the buggy would roll right over. No worries though, he'd roll it back over on its wheels and on he'd go.

A few changes were made when Ernie built his second dune buggy. A suspension that was more flexible is what he needed first. He figured a king pin in the front axle would allow the buggy to pivot side to side and would also allow both rear wheels to remain on the ground at all times for maximum pull.

Next, he welded the spider gears inside the rear end so that a quarter-turn is all they gave, creating a locked drive axle for greatest traction.

Ernie salvaged most of the parts from a '62 Ford Fairlane such as a 289 V-8 motor, 3-speed transmission, wheel hubs, and brake assemblies.

This new hill-climbing machine would go where 4-wheel drives only wished they could go. Together, Ernie and Daren would spend weekends having fun challenging the jeeps and other 4-wheel drives that were ignorant to what their 2-wheel drive, homemade machines could really do.

Ernie's buggy was fully restored in 2003. Now used as a neighborhood transportation vehicle and for an occasional Saturday romp up the mountains next to Ernie's home in Maricopa, Arizona.

Today, Ernie and Daren still enjoy sitting at the round table, reminiscing about the good old days when their homemade dune buggies dominated the mountains in south Phoenix, Arizona.

Chapter 2

"If You Build One, I'll Build One"

AS PHOENIX CONTINUED TO GROW IN POPULATION, the law eventually shut down the mountain trails, forbidding use of 4-wheelers and all motor vehicles on the rugged mountain trails. Ernie and Daren's dune buggy days came to an end.

It was about that same time in 1979 that Ernie, Daren and another fellow took their families on an outing to a 3-wheeled motorcycle side hack race at Phoenix International Raceway. During the drive home, Ernie expressed concern that 3-wheeled racers were too slow through the corners, and suggested that adding a car body would also help spectator appeal.

Ernie and Daren discussed the fact that only small portions of the race could be observed at one time. "An oval track would allow the spectators to see the whole race rather than one section," said Ernie.

After talking awhile and brain storming ideas, Ernie and Daren decided on a plan for the race cars. Daren told Ernie, "If you build one, I'll build one." Minutes later, the two were pulling parts out from Ernie's backyard and the Dwarf car phenomenon began.

Ernie decided his first would be the ever-popular 1934 Ford coup body style. Daren decided he would build a 1933 Dodge coup body. Both cars were built with a 73" wheelbase and 46" height. The little cars had all-steel construction and were powered by motorcycle engines.

Ernie had a 350cc Honda engine in his backyard he quickly put to use in his '34 Ford Dwarf. Daren was able to find a Kawasaki 350cc 3-cylinder, 2-stroke engine for his '33 Dodge Dwarf. The '34 Ford Dwarf was ready for a trial road test within a month. At that time, Daren's '33 Dodge Dwarf was halfway complete.

The first time the two Dwarf racers finally hit the track was March of 1981. Ernie and Daren were able to run a few hot laps around an eighth-mile dirt go-cart track by the name of Arrowhead Speedway in Phoenix. The cars were an instant attraction and the new Dwarf car racing class took off from there.

Top: **Ernie and Daren model the first two Dwarf cars before paint in 1980**

Bottom: **Ernie's 'Grumpy' and Daren's 'Doc' Dwarf cars are ready to race**

TANNER SCANNER

THE TANNER COMPANIES

OCTOBER/NOVEMBER/DECEMBER 1980

VOLUME 11, NO. 5

BEHIND THE SCENES

From Start...

To Finish.

IT'S A BIRD, IT'S A PLANE, NO, IT'S A DWARF CAR!

Ernie Adams, who is a Mechanic at Plant 4, started building the first "Dwarf Car" around January 1980. The idea came from watching motorcycle side back races. He always liked small cars so with this in mind he wanted to build a small race car.

The car is built from a wrecked or used motorcycle, light tubing and sheet metal which all cost under $1,000.00. Hoping that with a low cost, car interest could be generated by getting others interested in racing at a low cost.

The cars are equipped with a roll cage, proper regulation seat belts, fuel shut off valves, a chain guard and doors on both sides.

Thanks Ernie for sharing your hobby with us.

(Story contributed by Tom Vanderwalker.)

Ernie worked as a truck mechanic for Tanner Co. during his building of the Dwarf race cars in 1980. The Tanner Scanner was a company paper that ran the very first news article on the fascinating dwarfs.

As the Dwarfs' popularity increased, Ernie began to pump out the little race cars as fast as could be done in his small 10' x 12' shop, the original Dwarf car factory.

As people caught wind of the hot little racers, interest in the Dwarf cars grew quick. Ernie found himself waist-deep helping new Dwarf car enthusiasts build a car of their own. Each car was hand made of steel; most were fabricated right in Ernie's backyard.

As cars were finished one by one, anticipation grew for Dwarf car owners to put their hard work to a racetrack. It was suggested to trailer the racers to the open desert east of Phoenix and plow a makeshift track. The early Dwarf builders put a total of four different outings together, averaging five to eight cars. The eagerness of running a real race on a real track grew intensely each time the drivers climbed behind the wheel.

Left to right: Ernie Adams, Joe Corn, Dick Erickson, Kevin Adams, and Daren Schmaltz were among the Dwarf race car pioneers.

It was fall of 1983 when the first official Dwarf car race with a paid purse was booked. The venue, Yavapai County Fairgrounds in Prescott Arizona. The race event was scheduled as 'Demolition Derby and Dwarf Car Races,' Sunday, September 25, 1983.

As the sun shined down on the water soaked racetrack at the Yavapai County Fair, things began to look up for the excited Dwarf car racers. After heavy rain and flooding the first official Dwarf car race had come very close to cancellation.

The mud was deep and large puddles of water were throughout the racetrack. With the help of several volunteers, everyone worked Saturday and Sunday mornings, drying the track to make sure the show went on.

The crowd came alive when the Dwarf cars hit the track. People were amazed to see this new class of hot, little race cars. Ten cars were out of Phoenix and one car came from Prescott.

Ernie came out strong, winning the first heat race. Daren took first place in the next heat race, and Bobby "Bob" Rowe won the trophy dash and main event.

When the sun set low over the fairgrounds race track and all the cars had left, the memories and significance of that rainy day in Prescott will be forever remembered in car racing history. Thank you, Ernie, Daren and the nine other drivers for being a part of building a new racing class that would sweep the nation.

First official Dwarf car race at Yavapai County Fairgrounds, Prescott Arizona, September 1983

26

First Dwarf race car, 'GRUMPY,' after restoration in 2009

Ernie doing a few hot laps after restoration in his backyard in Maricopa, Arizona, 2009

Ernie Adams and his 'Big Bad Wolf' Dwarf race car.

When Ernie was asked, why he chose The Big Bad Wolf name, he replied, "Because I'm going to eat your ass up."

Chapter 3

Here To Stay

IT'S OCTOBER 3, 2011 AT 3:30 P.M., and I'm going to afternoon break time at my dad's garage a little early today. I packed my cooler with a six-pack of beer and stepped out the door. Today, I need another interview so I can move forward with my writings.

As I stepped inside the shop, Ernie paused his work and said, "Break time?" I explained to him my reason for an early arrival today. He says, "O.K." and heads for the refrigerator. As Ernie leans back in his big office chair, he puts his feet up and cracks a beer. My father has been patient with me and generous with his time while I get all the information I need. He takes a drink of his cold beer and his eyes roll toward the ceiling of his workshop, his mind working hard to recall the significant events I'm inquiring about today.

After interviewing my father and researching his colorful past, I, at times, feel as though I'm meeting him for the first time. My father enjoys talking. He'll always have a story to tell. If you listen close, you can find a lesson to be learned in each one.

Today I got lucky, no interruptions during my interview. I'm always trying to catch my dad at the perfect moment. Getting a minute or two of his time is quite difficult. There's most always someone visiting, or he'll be showing his cars. Often, I'll wait through five or six beers to get a five-minute interview—I don't mind the wait. That was a typical day before my decision to write this book.

I'm neither a writer nor a photographer. This has been an immense learning process for me. My dad is also learning to share his knowledge and life experiences in a way they can be captured by me to be immortalized in my writings for the entertainment of everyone.

The Dwarf cars were now growing to a level that some organization was needed. Dave Courtney, another Dwarf car owner, suggested it was time to form an association. A meeting was held at Dave's house; Ernie and Daren Schmaltz were in attendance. In this first meeting, the men discussed a clear plan for structuring the association.

After meeting with an attorney, elections for association officers were held. Ernie Adams was elected President, Daren Schmaltz Vice President, Sheila Adams Secretary-Treasurer, and Bob Rowe Race Coordinator. The Dwarf car bylaws were then drafted by Ernie Adams, Daren Schmaltz, Joe Corn, and Dave Courtney. These original bylaws are still used in today's Dwarf car association. The Legends race cars have since adopted those same bylaws. The first Legend race cars were simply a name change from 'Dwarf' to 'Legend,' and had fenders added to the Dwarf cars built off of Ernie's frame jigs.

Early Dwarf car builders had high hopes of someday having a race track to host Dwarf car racing. Ernie and Daren explored building an 1/8-mile dirt oval track specifically for racing them. They came across 8-½ acres of flood-prone desert northwest of Phoenix, listed at a price they could afford. Ernie and Daren thought this would be an ideal location to build their racetrack.

Plans for the track were drafted and submitted to the County Planning & Zoning Commission for a special-use permit. 'DWARF LAND SPEEDWAY' never made it far off the ground. Turned down by the County Board of Supervisors for building a race track, the Dwarf car owners looked for other avenues for racing their cars.

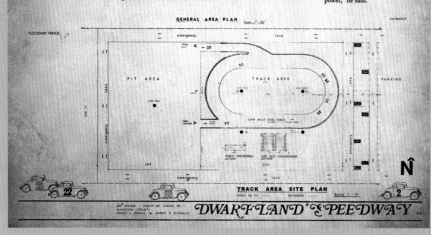

County gives 'dwarf car' race track black flag

Zoning stand leaves property owner with 'piece of river bottom'

By Ward Harkavy
Republic Staff

Dwarfland Speedway is dead.

It never got far off the ground, anyway.

Ernest E. Adams, trying to "get the ball rolling" for a new sport, wanted to build Arizona's first race track for "dwarf cars" — like the Big Bad Wolf, a waist-high imitation of a 1934 Ford coupe powered by a motorcycle engine.

His site, already purchased, was 8½ acres of flood-prone desert near 109th Avenue and Jomax Road next to the Agua Fria River and between Sun City and Lake Pleasant.

On Thursday, the Maricopa County Planning and Zoning Commission unanimously said no to Dwarfland Speedway after hearing opposition from county planners and from residents of the sparsely populated area.

Approval by the county Board of Supervisors seems unlikely.

"Now we're just stuck with a piece of river bottom," said Adams, a 43-year-old Phoenix mechanic and welder.

Carol Griffin, who lives on Jomax Road a few miles east of the site, wasn't sympathetic to Adams' request for a special-use permit.

"All the residents moved out here for one reason — quiet solitude," she told the commission.

Two other area residents voiced similar fears that a race track would produce too much noise and dust.

Adams vainly argued that the eighth-of-a-mile oval track would be recessed 3 feet into the ground to "dissipate" noise.

It was 20 years ago that Adams molded an old steel refrigerator into what he called "the granddaddy of dwarf cars."

It had too much power to be a Go Kart. And it wasn't a micromidget racer because it looked like a real car. So Adams dubbed it a "dwarf."

These days, dwarfs are made of sheets and tubes of steel, not old refrigerators. But some of the grilles on these miniature stock cars look suspiciously like the coolant coils from the backs of refrigerators.

Last year, for the Yavapai County Fair in Prescott, Adams helped put together the first real race for dwarf cars. Now, he said,

most of the state's 15 dwarf cars race in special features at big tracks like Firebird International Raceway, south of Phoenix.

But he said the sport needs more races — and the money to attract interest.

"A lot of guys like them, but they won't build one unless there's a place to run them," Adams said.

The purses at Firebird — only about $300 for the dwarfs — are as small as the cars. Adams said the sport could really grow if it had its own track, especially a small one designed for the little cars.

Most of his free time is spent scrounging parts to help others build dwarfs, Adams said, because of the growing interest in the sport. "They're chockful of horse power," he said.

The Arizona Republic, April 6, 1984

South of Phoenix, a new dirt oval race track named Firebird International Raceway opened its gates. The Dwarf cars were offered a $300 purse to run a special feature on the quarter-mile track. At this time, 15 cars were race-ready throughout Arizona.

It wasn't long before three other tracks were willing to make a place for the fast-growing Dwarf cars. Once prospective car builders knew they had a place to run a car, the Dwarf car craze exploded. They had made their mark and it was apparent they were here to stay.

During this boom, a man by the name of John Cain befriended Ernie. John had a wealth of knowledge in racing these cars as the full size real deal in their hay day. He began helping Ernie in his backyard shop on weekends. John understood the direction Ernie was steering the Dwarf cars and the association. He liked what Ernie was doing and wanted to help the cars succeed. Ernie had up to 12 new cars and frames at one time in his small backyard. Soon, it was apparent the operation had outgrown the small space.

DWARFS

The Dwarf Car began with the idea of Ernie Adams and Darin Schmaltz a few years ago. The association itself is just now taking off with many eager members ready to help anyone interested in a Dwarf Car, with advice, tips and technical information.

With the nostalgic look, as in early stock car racing, the cars 1928 to 1948 American vintage style coupes and sedans, are powered by any motorcycle engine. Cars are only 38" tall and can be chain, shaft or belt drive. The idea is to have a car, racing enthusiasts can still afford to build and be competed with. Many of the components can be bought, prefab from Ambrooke Motor Cars, Inc. in Prescott or if you prefer Allan Neff and his crew there, will build your favorite style car scaled down to Dwarf Car size.

THE DRIVERS, THEIR CARS, THEIR SPONSORS

CAR # / NAME / TYPE OF CAR / DRIVER / CITY / SPONSOR

00 "Sylvester"/34 Chev. Sedan/Gail Summers/Ams Oil/ Phoenix
03 "Woody Woodpecker"/32 Ford 3 Window Coupe/ Jim Barker/Salvage Auto Parts/Phoenix
2 "Road Runner"/33 Dodge Coupe/John Courtney Phoenix
4 "Tasmainian Devil"/32 Chevy 5 Window Coupe/ Dennis Martin/Chino Valley

6 /39 Chevy Coupe/John Cain/Stohl's Beer/Tempe
9 "Woody Woodpecker"/29 Ford Sedan/John Wilson/ Prescott
14 "Sleepy"/30 Ford 5 Window Coupe/Kim Henager/ Prescott
17 "Speedy Gonzales"/32 Chevy 5 Window Coupe/ Daren Schmaltz/Phoenix

24 "Big Bad Wolf"/34 Ford Sedan/Ernest Adams/Mesa Drive Shaft/Phoenix
29 "Fred Flintstone"/34 Chevy Sedan/Bob Dowe/Dial Rentals/Apache Jct.
29X /30 Ford Sedan/Ben Henegar/Prescott
34 "Grumpy"/George Meikle/Phoenix

38 "Casper the Friendly Ghost/Ambrooke Motor Car Co./Dave "Spooky" Doty/Prescott
40 "Snoopy"/30 Ford 5 Window Coupe/Richard Erickson/US Rents/Glendale
49 "Yosemite Sam"/32 Chevy 5 Window Coupe/Allan Neff Ambrooke Metal Craft/Ambrooks Car Co./Prescott
69 "Garfield"/40 Ford Coupe/Ron Christensen/Prescott

Continued-top of next page

42

77 "Grumpy"/32 Ford 5 Window Coupe/George Thompson/ Prescott
Mr. "T"/32 Ford Vicki Sedan/Jerry Watson/ Prescott

1984 RULES

BODY

1. There will be only one class of cars.
2. Car body will be of 1928 to 1948 vintage; coupe or sedan.
3. No open cars such as roadsters or convertibles.
4. Foreign makes, panels or pickups.
5. Will be of all metal construction. No fiber glass.
6. No fenders front or rear.
7. Doors and windows must remain in stock appearance. Right and left doors must be operational. Right door only may be shortened a maximum of 4" from the bottom up. For header or exhaust pipe only.
8. Each car will have grill shell or simulated open radiator matching body style.
9. Engine compartment must conform to original as to scale of body.
10. No engine transmission assembly may extend to rear more than 21" from center of front axle, except separate transmission where transmission may be mounted in place of jackshaft, i.e. Harley.
11. Front bumper no wider than 24" and should not extend more than 6" forward of front tires.
12. Rear bumper no wider than 50" and should not exceed 6" from extreme rear body panel.
13. No body shall be over 38" tall from bottom of outer edge to extreme top, including frame rail. No body shall be over 46" tall from ground up to extreme top.
14. No body prior to 1940 including 1940 shall exceed 36" in width. No body 1941 or later shall exceed 38" in width.
15. All bodies must have trunk lid or truck access panel as to conform to original body lines.

CLEAN APPEARANCE

16. Front suspension must not exceed tire height or extend rearward past the most forward panel of the firewall, except under frame rail where it cannot be seen from either side. All steering mechanisms must have safety fasteners such as cotter pins or self locking nuts.
   No rear suspension shall be mounted or extend outside car's natural body lines, including frame rail. Kickouts must be mounted in front of the rear axle only. A maximum of 18" from axles to kickout. Also must be a three point mounting no more than 16" to center of both lower mounting points, and the upper mount no more than 18" above bottom of frame rail or lowest point. Kickouts must not extend out to either side past the tire tread.
17. Exhaust and headers must be installed as not to distract from a stock appearing hood, with the exception of side panels.
18. No glass of any kind will be permitted. A 1/2 inch square mesh windscreen is required.

FASTENERS

19. Door latches, right and left sides must be a standard gate latch only, on all cars. Inside mount only.
20. Hood and trunk access panels must be fastened securely by spring latch, bolt and nut, or dzus fasteners. (No self tapping screws)

Continued-top of next page

43

Firebird's Official Program For The 1984 Racing Season

"A hobby out of control," a term which aptly describes the Dwarf Car craze around the Arizona race tracks these days. What began as a past-time seven years ago, fashioned with a couple discarded refrigirators, a busy torch and an even busier imagination, all in repertoire of one Ernie Adams of Phoenix has gathered his friends, John Proctor and John Cain, and moved out of backyard into a modern facility complete with office, sheet metal and fenced lot. Stripped of the "hobby" disguise this "idea" now keeps the three partners and several helpers hardpressed for time enough to fill the demans coming in the for these hard charging, handmade, little speed burners.

—Our Town Magazine
"A Hobby Out of Control"

John Cain and another Dwarf car driver, John Proctor presented to Ernie the idea of going into business together. After contemplating awhile, Ernie agreed to enter a three-way partnership with both men. As equal partners, they would move into a more accommodating facility, were the business could thrive. At this time, Ernie had enough frame jigs to build 18 different body styles. The decision for a company name was not hard. They simply called it the 'Dwarf Car Co.'

The new business was an immediate success. Now Dwarf car enthusiast had a place to buy a car at any stage of completion they desired. Repairs, modifications, and a full line of parts were the services offered. Dwarf car sales were all word of mouth and did well.

Dwarf car building became more and more innovative as the company moved forward. New jigs were created to make wheels and elaborate hoods. The company began making instructional videos on suspensions and steering assemblies.

By 1987, Dwarf cars were featured at most all of Arizona's major dirt tracks, and the cars began stretching outside the Arizona boarders. Dwight Dietrich and Bob Knisler of Kansas got word of the hot little cars and purchased four complete Dwarf bodies with plans of starting a new chapter in Kansas.

An invitation to run an exhibition race in Juárez, Mexico was accepted by the Dwarf cars Association. Twenty-two race cars were escorted threw Juárez to a track where they put on a fascinating show for the Mexican people.

Ernie prepares the new 'Big Bad Wolf' for hauling ass.

The premier season of Ernie's second 'Big Bad Wolf'

In the summer of 1988, Ernie and John Cain loaded up their Dwarf cars and headed out across the Midwest. Their destination was Ohio. Stopping along the way in Red Cloud Nebraska, Ernie and John were able to get on the local dirt track and run an exhibition race. They picked up $100.00 for the exciting show the Dwarf cars put on.

Traveling on, the cute little cars attracted attention everywhere they went. At times, stopping for a bite to eat or fueling the trucks would turn into a timely event. People would frequently stop to inquire about the unusual little cars.

Once the Dwarfs reached Ohio, Ernie and John put on another special feature for race fans on Saturday night in Bowling Greens. Due to a tangle in the turn between Ernie and John, the cars were incapacitated and not able to finish the show.

As interest in the Dwarf cars grew at an astonishing rate, Ernie began to see the quality of the cars' authenticity diminish. Cars not up to specs were showing up to races, expecting to run. Ernie was adamant that cars not meeting all specifications and safety requirements in accordance with the Dwarf car bylaws would not race, but each time, these illegal cars were permitted to race by the inspector. This became an escalating problem, leading up to Ernie's dissolution of his partnership in the Dwarf Car Co.

Ernie is a detailed person that knew a Dwarf car body's authenticity was the magic in creating the Dwarf car craze; the distinction that put the dwarfs in a class of their own.

In 1989, Ernie decided it was time for him to move on. He had given all he could possibly give to the creation and evolution of the Dwarf race cars. Just as a grown child leaving home for the first time, Ernie raised them from the beginning, and now it's time to step back and let the Dwarfs grow on their own.

Ernie sold his frame jigs to 'Brunson, Miller, and Davis', who went on to establish Dwarf Cars Unlimited. After 10 challenging years of building the cars, it was not the end for Ernie but, in fact, the beginning of a whole new chapter for the Dwarfs.

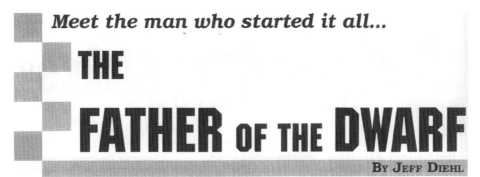

Meet the man who started it all...

THE
FATHER OF THE DWARF

BY JEFF DIEHL

Ernie Adams in his home-based and home-style car garage.

Dwarf Car Racer, 1992

Chapter 4

"Precious Memory"

A MOVE IN A NEW DIRECTION. Out of the dirt and onto the street. In 1989, Ernie made his transition. The Dwarf race cars' popularity had risen to a level to which they could grow on their own. The cars were running on major tracks in 17 states. Evolving further each season, the cars were faster and more exciting than ever. Ernie's creativity had been bottled up for the past 10 years; his originality was especially limited with the Dwarf race cars. Now, Ernie wanted to build a real car, a Dwarf car that was street-legal.

Back to where the Dwarf cars began, he cleared the small area in front of his tiny backyard shop in Phoenix, and commenced to plan his masterpiece.

December 26, 2011: Late getting to 4:30 break time, I pulled up to my dad's garage and parked among four other cars and two quads. I could see the smoke bellow from the tall, steel chimney, which is always an indication my dad is here. As I walked in from the December cold to a hot fire roaring inside the old iron wood stove, the group was happy to see I had made it. Ernie was in his usual place, his feet up and leaning far back in his big office chair. I had to ask, 'Did you get any work done today'? "Nope," he said, "been visiting all day." It's not uncommon for Ernie to have several visitors on Saturdays. As one group's leaving, another is driving in. Some are astonished to see Ernie's living museum for the first time.

After a few drinks, I hear the sound of an engine starting. It's 6:00 p.m., according to the Ford clock on the wall. At the top of every hour, the sound of a different Ford engine sounds. Break time's over. Everyone knows that at 6:00 Ernie's due inside for dinner.

January 12, 2012: I grabbed my camera and a cold beer then hopped on my old, three-wheel motorbike. Down the back road I drove to my dad's shop. Today, I need more details on his Dwarf '39 Chevy. I had hoped to get in and out in a timely manner but I might of known that's never an easy task. When I pulled up, Ernie and three friends were enjoying a bullshit session just inside the big, steel sliding doors. The warm sun was shining inside the door and an empty chair was close by, so I claimed the chair and listened in on today's gossip. After a beer or two Ernie's company moved on. It was my turn for some one-on-one time with him. I handed him a picture of his Dwarf '39 Chevy and played 20 questions. I asked him to take me back to the beginning, back to the starting point, and walk me through the process to which he put this car together. He held the picture in his rough, grease-stained hands and stared for a moment, his mind working to recall the process from 21 years ago. After a moment of silence, he said, "Well, I started with a picture of the car I wanted to build. I took measurements from the picture, and then I built the car freehand. Next, I set up the motor, transmission and rear end to fit the length and width of the car. The Toyota rear axle had to be cut and narrowed to size also. The front axle was custom-built. Ernie paused for a sip of beer and then continued.

I used 12"-wheels and customized them to resemble the original American wheels. From there, I built the lower frame within the drivetrain in a manner that accommodated the steering sector, seating and fuel tank. At this point, I begin to build a birdcage-type of frame and form the sheet steel around that frame to make the car body. After the doors were fabricated, I moved onto the bumpers, front grille, sun visor and fender skirts. Last, was the electric, chrome and paint.

Ernie started construction of this car in 1990. He spent two and a half years from start to finish. This car is a solid 1,770 lbs. and can cruse at highway speeds with ease. Ernie's Dwarf 1939 Chevy has been on the road for 17 years and has 57,000.00 miles on it to date.

Sounds easy enough, right? Not exactly; a person would be amazed at the hours, determination and hard work Ernie put into building a car like this. Aside from the Toyota drivetrain, every last piece of the car is completely handcrafted from flat steel.

Here, Ernie has finished the frame. The motor, transmission, and rear end have been mounted. Next, he'll go to work on the firewall that covers the transmission, and building the floorpan all the way to the rear of the car.

With the floorpan and suspension finished, Ernie set the fuel tank and built the body. Next, he'll build the doors and trunk hood.

Here, you see a primitive front grille before being tailored and chromed. The hood is ready to cut openings for the louvers. The body is done and primed at this point.

Ernie built the front fenders by forming the sheet metal around a temporary frame that was removed after the fenders were finished. Remember, there's no fiberglass or plastic in the car body. The running boards are attached and the rear fenders are next.

You can see Ernie's work, as he built the rear fenders. One piece of steel was attached with two splits in it. They were welded together and dollied out round. Then, two more pieces were added in the same manner to finish the front of the fender. The framework was then removed, leaving only the fender.

The body and fenders are complete. Now the car is ready for the hood louvers, glass and wiring. Last, Ernie made all the trimming such as bumpers, sun visor and fender skirts. When completed, the entire car was disassembled in preparation of the final primer and paint.

January 15, 2012: The sun is high and bright on this beautiful Saturday afternoon. A great day to visit my dad's Dwarf car shop and see if I can get some information on his little 1939 Chevy.

I grabbed a six-pack of beer and hopped in my old truck. I drove down the back dirt road and into Ernie's long drive way. Disappointed to see that Ernie's truck was gone, I pulled in and parked anyway. As I clicked my door open, Ernie drove up and beeped his horn. Around to the backside of his shop he goes, pulling a trailer loaded with scrap steel. My chances of getting some much-needed information today suddenly increased.

As Ernie and I took our seats at the round table I could hear the sound of quads. Ernie's at home and the whole neighborhood seems to know it. First one quad, then another, and shortly after comes one more. My mom stepped out from the house and headed for the shop as my brother, Rick, rounded the drive at the same time. And just like déjà vu, it's break time again at Ernie's.

The round table conversation usually follows the topic of cars or machines of some sort. Ernie will often reminisce about the good old days of dune buggy riding and the early days of Dwarf car racing. I recall quite a conversation between Ernie and friend, Roger Lane, on the difference between the trunk doors of a 1948 Chevy and a 1940 Buick. Ernie enjoys a good conversation, as much as building his cars.

When break time was over, just as they came, one by one the visitors left. This was my window of opportunity to get a one-on-one interview with Ernie.

Today, I'll ask him about the many adventures he and his Dwarf 1939 Chevy have embarked on. The shop is quite and Ernie leans back in his chair as his big, fat cat, Amber, takes a place on his lap.

Ernie begins: "Early on around 1992, one of my first road trips was driving from Phoenix to Pomona, California for the hot rod show and swap meet." He goes on to tell the story of driving into the show and parking his car along with the street rods. Several people approached him. "We don't think you should park here," they said. "We think you need to park down among the Volkswagens." Ernie grinned as he went on with his story. "It didn't make a difference to me where I parked," said Ernie. As he headed toward the Volkswagens, two men stopped Ernie and visited a bit. "Those guys said I should park down by the Volkswagens," Ernie told the men. "Hell, park right in here with us," they told Ernie. One guy had a 1934 Ford pickup, and the other one had a 1955 Plymouth

To the street rodders' surprise, Ernie's Dwarf car drew the attention of several viewers that day. He was informed later that he was noted in a car magazine from another country on his day in Pomona.

Left — See what we mean about cruisin'?
Right — No, that's not an 8-foot street rodder, rather a 4-foot '39 Chevy two-door. Ernest Adams drove it up from Phoenix, Arizona; Ernest built it himself to about 2/3 scale. Word has it he's working on another one, too! Absolutely amazing workmanship in this thing.

Ernie's Dwarf 1939 Chevy during attendance of the GoodGuys Heartland Nationals in Des Moines, Iowa 1992
RODDER'S DIGEST

Late in June of 1992, Ernie packed his '39 Chevy Dwarf and set off for Des Moines, Iowa. This would be the big test for his little car. Leaving from Phoenix, Ernie would travel approximately 1,600 miles one way and cross over six state lines to get there.

This year would be the first time the Goodguys venture into the upper Midwest and hold their Heartland Rod & Custom Nationals at the Iowa State Fairgrounds. Ernie showed up in a very small way. With more than 25,000 spectators that weekend, Ernie's car had many of them scratching their heads, with queer looks on their faces.

From there, he went on to Lincoln, Nebraska to meet up with the end of R&C'S third annual Americruise. It was there that Ernie met a little person named Sonny Ross. For such a little man, he had big words for Ernie calling his car a Dwarf, but complimented him on a nice article he had read on Ernie's Dwarf '39 Chevy.

In 1993, Ernie drove his little '39 Chevy in the Arizona Route 66 Fun Run as a first-time participant in a three-day event stretching 1,000 miles roundtrip. He's continued to run the Route 66 now for 16 years. Ernie drives his car the entire trip and also does plenty of cruising along with the big cars. He gives a lot of rides and poses for many pictures too.

Probably the most unusual car at the Cruise was Ernest Adams' '50s-style, itty-bitty '39 Chevy two-door sedan from Phoenix. Note the road rash; Adams' lilliputian lowrider is a driver.

No you're not seeing things. The fellow leaving this '39 Chevy sedan isn't "Andre the Giant"! The '39 is a perfect miniature of a Chevy sedan in every detail...check out the Malibu in the background. Trick, huh!

Route 66 Fun Run in 2005. Here, Ernie was featured in 'Tales of the emerald Chevy,' by Greg Brown in Flight Training magazine.

Opposite Side, Left to Right:

Ernie at R&C's third annual Americruise in Lincoln, Nebraska, 1992, HOT ROD magazine
Ernie on his first annual Route 66 Fun Run in Arizona, 1993, STEETSCENE magazine

FUJI RDPIII

Chapter 5

"April Love"

ERNIE'S '39 CHEVY WAS NO DOUBT A ONE-OF-A-KIND, BIG SUCCESS. Pleased with the fan feedback and show reviews, Ernie couldn't wait to build another work of genius. In an early interview, I asked him how he decided what body style to use for the next Dwarf cruiser. "April Love," said Ernie, followed by a short pause.

I turned my head with a puzzled look on my face, and he continued: "In 1957, I watched a picture show called 'April Love,'" The movie featured a baby-blue 1942 Ford Deluxe convertible. "I fell in love with that car," Ernie said. "That's the car I wanted to build!" He went on to say, "I like the grille and the convertible feature of the '42 Ford compared to the '46, '47 and '48 Fords."

It was 1992, when Ernie began construction on his new Dwarf '42 Ford. Beginning with a picture of the full-sized '42, he took all the measurements needed. Unlike the Dwarf '39 Chevy, he built a jig to construct the frame with. In the small area in front of his workshop, he set the engine in place and laid out the frame rails. From there, he made a front straight-axle suspension. In the rear, he narrowed a Toyota axle to size and mounted it on the frame. The floorpan followed, and then the framing for the body. Ernie continued building a dream into reality.

Creating the Dwarf '39 Chevy brought Ernie's steel fabricating abilities to a much higher level then they'd ever been before. He had learned to bend and shape steel, just as a sculpture could mold a lump of clay into a beautiful work of art.

New challenges appeared as the little car began to take shape. This car had a transverse leaf spring and required a torque tube to restrict the axle from twisting. A wishbone was used in the front suspension, which created a problem with the oil pan. The sump of the oil pan needed to be changed from the front to the rear to allow the engine to set correctly over the axle.

"When I built the body, I had to figure out how to get the convertible top to fold down in between the rear fenders," said Ernie. The continental kit needed to fold out in a manner that the trunk could open and close freely without the spare tire in its way. These are some of the very real situations that Ernie had to surmount when building a whole car from flat steel.

Tuesday morning 11:15 a.m., my telephone rings once, then twice; I answer on the third ring.

"Grab your camera and get over here," said my mom. "There's a line of cars heading up the drive." I abruptly hung up the phone and headed out the door, camera in hand. Sliding around the corner into the long dirt drive up to Ernie's big, steel building. I didn't want to miss any photo opportunities.

As I neared the old building, I could see cars everywhere. I found a small parking spot and quickly went inside the shop. I didn't get far before I ran into a wall of people. The crowed stood in a large circle around one of Ernie's little cars as he commentated on all the details involved in the fabrication of the car. I wasted no time snapping shots of the mesmerized circle of viewers. I politely pushed my way by the onlookers and up the stairway onto the loft. From there, I could capture the event from a bird's-eye view.

The spare tire folds up and out, allowing the trunk hood to open and close freely.

I took a rough count of around 17 cars and approximately 35 guests. Ernie had his hands full with answering questions fired at him one after another about his cars. "Let's see you get inside one, Ernie," said a man, who was ready to capture the event with his camera.

After a full tour of the Dwarf Car factory, just as they arrived, the cars all loaded up. A wave goodbye and a thank you from each as they headed out the drive one by one.

Ernie grabbed himself a cold beer and headed for the round table. He sat back in his old office chair and lifted his scuffed cowboy boots upon another chair. Parched from talkng nonstop, he pulled the tab on the cold High Life beer, draws a long drink and simply says, "Yep, that was quite a crowd."

Ernie finished up his Dwarf '42 Ford in 1999. After seven years, his weekend hobby had taken shape as a beautiful, baby-blue, half-pint convertible. It had all the beauty and class of the Dwarf '39, but it was stunning in so many other ways.

Excited about the completion of his new car, Ernie wanted to get out and show the world. The Pavilions in Scottsdale, Arizona is where the new little Ford debuted. When Ernie entered the show, a growing crowd of onlookers suddenly began to follow behind him as he drove through the show and found a place to park. Like bugs to a porch light, people gathered around the car and gazed in amazement. Sometimes seeing is not believing, "I couldn't believe how many pictures were taken that night," said Ernie. "People really loved the car!"

Inside the door of each one of Ernie's cars,
you will find a steel tag bearing his engraved signature

"When I built my '42 Dwarf, I wanted to drive it on a cross-country road trip," said Ernie. In 2003, he signed up for the Mid-Americruise. The cruise would begin in Wauconda, Illinois and run all the way to Lincoln, Nebraska. On a hot June morning, Ernie packed his small suitcase and left his home in Phoenix. His adventure took him through northern Arizona and into New Mexico. From there, he crossed the panhandle of Texas and into Oklahoma. It took a full day's drive up the middle of Kansas to his hometown of Harvard, Nebraska where he proudly showed off his car to family and friends.

The next day. Enie was on his way again. He crossed Nebraska and then Iowa up into Illinois until he reached Wauconda.

Starting at Hides Rod Shop, approximately 35 cars headed out across the Midwestern open highway for Lincoln, Nebraska where the main show was hosted. The cars made stops in small towns and different rod shops along the way. "Any time I would pull over, I had a one-man car show," said Ernie. People would gather around the car and wonder what they're looking at. Four or five cars would drop off along the way and then four or five would join in. "We still had about 35 cars when we pulled into Lincoln," said Ernie. There, he received the Rod & Custom Magazine Editor's Choice award for 2003.

January 2004 • Rod & Custom **31**

fixin's. 7 No, your eyes aren't playing tricks on you—it's a "dwarf" '42 Ford convertible! The all-steel, Toyota-powered rod was hand-fabricated by its owner, Ernest Adams *(middle)*, who drove from Phoenix to Chicago before cruising with us to Lincoln. We gave it the *Car We Want To Drive Home* award.

Rod & Custom Magazine, January 2004

One afternoon, my father, Ernie ,and I were visiting over a few cold beers. I had to ask him, "How many miles have you put on this little convertible?" After a short pause and a look back into his mind, he said, "I don't know exactly how many miles I've driven this car. It's been on the Arizona Route 66 Fun Run four years now. Each year adds up another thousand miles because it's driven the whole way without a chase car." From the gravel-pitted paint to the half-worn tires, it's plain to see this car was not built as a trailer queen.

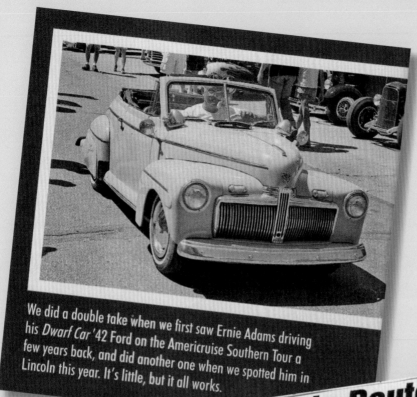

We did a double take when we first saw Ernie Adams driving his *Dwarf Car '42 Ford* on the Americruise Southern Tour a few years back, and did another one when we spotted him in Lincoln this year. It's little, but it all works.

**Rod & Custom Magazine,
December 2007**

**New Zealand
RODDER Magazine,
ISSUE 14**

Historic Route 66 revisited

• No, Ernst isn't a giant. He drove 200 miles to the fun run in his 5/8 scale Merc that runs a 1200cc Toyota. It took 4000 hours over seven years to build, with only photos to work from.

Ernie and Sheila stand beside the Dwarf 1942 Ford.
Ernie loved the '60s song 'Sheila' and wanted to honor his wife of
50 years by naming his car 'Sweet Little Sheila'. He's proud to show
it off on the rear fender skirt of his baby-blue cruiser.

Here, Ernie Proudly models his 1942 Dwarf in Maricopa, Arizona.

Ernie at age 19, stands next to his 1949 Chevy convertible.
As a young man, he went by his middle name, Eily.

chapter 6

Half Moon Rd

DUST WHIRLS UP AND AROUND THE BACK OF THE CAR as Ernie and friend Roger Lane drive down the desolate dirt road south of Phoenix. Along they drive, past a lizard and a rattlesnake searching through the tall saguaros for that perfect piece of property. What started with an early morning surprise phone call from Roger Lane soon became a whole new beginning for Ernie and the future of his Dwarf car ventures.

It was a warm April Saturday morning when Roger decided to get Ernie out of the house. "Come on," Roger told Ernie. "Let's go out and find a piece of property." Roger's original idea was to find a place for one big building that Roger, Ernie and another fellow could split three ways. Ernie wasn't easily convinced on this plan. "I'd like to buy my own land and build my own building," he told Roger.

The sun slowly pushed across the clear, blue sky and hung low above the tall mountains south of Maricopa. Unimpressed with any properties they had looked at, Ernie abruptly said, "STOP!" "Back up" he tells Roger as he points his finger to a street sign. "Half Moon Road," Ernie reads out loud. Next to that stood another sign advertising two 10-acre lots for sale. Roger turned the wheel and steered the car down the narrow, rugged dirt road. When the car began to drag the bottom, Sheila said, "I'm not living here." Let's get out and take a look around, Ernie suggested. This is a beautiful piece of land, he thought to himself. "I'd be interested in getting these two lots if they're available. I'll buy one and you buy the other," Ernie said to Roger. A contract was negotiated at $27,000 for both lots and the two men signed their names on the dotted line.

Ernie had two years left to work his job as a truck mechanic before he could retire. The plan was to retire and then move to his new property. That plan soon went right out the window when his friend Leroy told him about a building for sale. Much different from the 10' x 12' workshop he was used to, this building was 60' x 40' and 21' tall. The big steel building sat on the corner of Central Avenue, one block south of Buckeye Road in Phoenix. Ernie gave $2,000 for the old structure and it was his responsibility to move it. This fellow, Leroy, had a crew of men working for him. He and his crew worked along with Ernie on disassembling the big steel giant. The main beams were all welded together as one solid structure. "In order to transport the beams, I had to cut each one into four separate pieces," said Ernie. Working two trailer loads at a time, slowly, the building made it to its new home in Maricopa.

The first step in reassembling the building was to weld the large steel beams together again. Ernie welded one side of all beams first. With the use of a rented backhoe, he dug holes and dragged the main beams across the holes while lifting them up and over with the bucket. Next, he stacked them in a manner he could weld the other sides, one right after another.

THE MAIN BEAMS

BEGINNING TO TAKE SHAPE

With the use of his homemade gin pole, Ernie raised the heavy main beams upright and bolted them into place. From there, the old building began to take shape. With its blemished steel panels and rustic appearance, the building already had a personality of its own. When Ernie and his Dwarf cars were added, the dusty road to nowhere soon became The Road to Wonder.

February 24, 2013: After a particularly long winter, spring began to shine upon our rural desert neighborhood. The light-green pampas grass carpeted the desert floor and the cacti were beginning to bloom. My friend Bonnie and I spent the early afternoon on a scenic dune buggy ride across the tall mountains that stretch behind our houses. On the way home, we turned in on Half Moon Road. We could see Ernie's shop doors were open and he was working out front. Though not quite 4:30 break time yet, we decided to stop in and say hi. I cranked the wheel and stepped on the gas, giving the buggy a nice slide into Ernie's long driveway. When we got around the corner, headed for the shop, we could see that Ernie was at it again. He had an old cement mixer out front and was cutting it apart with his torch. "What are you doing with that?" I had to ask. "I'm making a white wall machine," Ernie replied. He strikes the torch and cuts another bar from the old mixer. We watched as the orange and blue flame seared through the steel bar. He finished the cut, then turned the gas off. With a loud snap, the flame disappeared and he sat the torch down. He pointed to the drive gear that was still attached to the motor. "The wheel will mount in a manner so it will rest upon this gear. The drive gear will turn the wheel and allow me to evenly apply the white wall resin."

ERNIE'S WHITE WALL MACHINE

Ernie learned to be resourceful at an early age. Growing up in a poor family, along with five other siblings, buying things new from a store was unheard of. As a young man, he lived just three blocks from the Harvard City dump. "I would walk a gravel road along the railroad tracks down to the dump," said Ernie. "Almost anything we needed we found right there at that dump. We would get our furniture, electric motors, scrap iron, bicycle parts, and wheels of all sorts," he added.

As he grew older he continued to salvage anything of value: scrap steel, engines and building materials. I had to ask my father, "What is it with old refrigerators you were always collecting?" "I would find old refrigerators and sell the freezing units for the green brass. The refrigerators were always good, useable steel to work with," he explained.

When Ernie moved to Phoenix in 1971, he had only 11' to work with behind his house. With little room for storage in his small 9' x 13'-workshop, he found the multiuse of refrigerators also made for great parts storage that fit nicely in the small area behind his house.

Ernie brought his refrigerator collection along with him when he relocated to the Town of Maricopa. If you look at Ernie's refrigerators, they bear a striking resemblance to another world wonder.

Ernie's refrigerator collection   **Stonehenge (England)**

When Ernie needs a piece of steel, he usually doesn't need to look any further than his own backyard. "I save everything I can and I buy my steel at bargain prices. I'll always have a use for it," he says.

Being resourceful often leads Ernie to his scrap pile.
Like all good pack rats, Ernie had just the thing he was
looking for; it was a split-metal rod with symmetrical bends
at the end that seemed to have been put there in the distant
past by Providence for just what he needed.

Tuesday May 3: Today, I scheduled a vacation day from my real job.
The word is, a couple of guys from Phoenix are heading out here to present
Ernie with an idea for filming a documentary on him and his Dwarf cars. "The
guys from Phoenix will be here at 9:00 tomorrow morning," Ernie told me as I

left his shop the night before. "Bring your camera and computer," he added.

Eight o'clock the next morning my phone rings; it's my mother. "The guys from Phoenix will be here in 10 minutes," she said. Typical for me, one phone call turns 9:00 am to 8:00 am in an instant. Wasting no time, I picked up my camera and grabbed my laptop, then ran out the door as it slammed shut behind me. In a rush, I turned my truck key and released the clutch. With a spin of the tires and a puff of dust, I hurried over to Ernie's. My plan was to have my cameras in place when the men arrived and catch the meeting on film.

Just minutes later. I arrived and pulled off to the side, careful not to block any camera view of the building. The big steel doors were cracked open enough that I could turn sideways and squeeze inside. Once inside, I found a clear spot on a workbench and opened my camera bag. I'm too late; a Nissan Pathfinder rolls up and stops in front of the old gas pumps. I could hear the sound of two car doors close. Ernie opens the side door, "We're in here," he shouts. Seconds later, two young men walk inside and up a short hallway. Just inside clear view, the first guy stops abruptly. "This is it," he says. Eyes open wide and a pleased look on his face, he says to his partner, "We can defiantly do something with this!" Ernie extends his hand and introduces himself, then me. "I'm Charlie, the writer, and this is my cameraman, Mike," one said with a return handshake. Still standing just inside the room, Charlie comments again, "Amazing!"

"Come in and let me show you around," Ernie says. After a show and tell on all the cars, the next two hours were spent going through videos, pictures and magazine articles. Mike the cameraman was of few words, but I could read his expressions of deep thought. "Ernie, you amaze me more and more," Charlie said after hearing fascinating stories of the Dwarf car saga. Satisfied with all they've experienced, the two men stood up and, again, extended their hands. With a handshake, Charlie said, "Ernie, we love what you're doing and we would be honored to tell the world your story." On that note, the two men walked out the door, climbed into their truck, and drove away.

chapter 7

"16" AND "STILL" SINGLE

LISTEN CLOSE AND YOU CAN ALMOST HEAR THE PLUGGING OF A WHISKY JUG, a banjo playing, and a set of spoons slapping on a knee. You walk around once, twice and then again, scratching your head. With each walk around, you spot something you missed the first time around.

Perhaps one of Ernie's most interesting Dwarf cars is a scaled 1929 Ford Model A 'Hillbilly' car. It's one thing to be able to build cars such as the Dwarf '39 Chevy or a Dwarf '42 Ford, fully dressed in beautiful paint, but this time Ernie stepped outside the box. Remembering back to his hillbilly roots on the back roads of Nebraska, he found inspiration in a man he met in Des Moines, Iowa. He tells the story of how he'd attended a car show and one car in particular caught his eye. "The owner called himself Hillbilly Bob and he had an old '29 Ford Model A," said Ernie. "I watched him kick the tire and the car started. The engine chugged and the car shook with puffs of smoke coming from the exhaust." Ernie continued, "There was an old bed frame strapped on the running board and various trinkets of all kinds attached to the body. I walked around the car two or three times looking at all the quirky attachments," he said.

In January 2000, Ernie attended a car show at the Pinal County Fairgrounds in Casa Grande, Arizona. It was here that Ernie met a man named Zeek from Missouri. Similar to Hillbilly Bob's car in Iowa, Zeek had an old Model A sedan and his wife had a tattered Model A coupe. "When I saw the cars, I had to walk right over and take a look," said Ernie. Zeek wore bib overalls with patches sewn on the knees. On his head was a floppy, wide-brimmed hat pulled up in the center and pinned to the top. His wife was fully clad in a hand-sewn flowered dress, boots and a straw hat with several flowers attached. Zeek's sedan had a gabled roof with the pitch of a backwoods cabin. In the center of the roof stood a weather vane with a rooster on top. Pots, pans, tools and many other ornaments hung from the car's body.

"I like your cars," Ernie told the man. "I like to build small, homemade cars and I'd like to build a hillbilly Dwarf car," he added.

Saturday morning, I poured myself a cup of coffee and took a seat in front of my kitchen window. The sun glistened off the morning dew upon the wilting grass blades. I can feel the chill of a cold December morning coming from the window. I take a sip of my coffee and allow my mind to wonder. I have so many different directions in which this hillbilly chapter could go. I sit here in my chair with a hypnotized stare out the window, pondering how to put it all together. As I gulped the last of my coffee it came to me; I need to go to the source.

I slipped on my boots, grabbed my camera bag, and a pad of paper on my way out the door. My truck window had a light cover of frost across it so I hit the wiper switch to clear it away. I thought to myself, I hope Ernie has the old wood stove fired up, catching a chill down my spine as I thought about the warm fire.

Happy to see smoke rolling from the chimney, I walked in to find my dad sitting right where I thought he'd be. Ernie was leaning back in his big office chair with his fat cat, Amber, stretched across his lap. His long legs stretch out and perched upon an old bucket in front of the stove. "Good morning," he said holding his green coffee cup. I sat down close to the fire and told him I was here to do some writing. He began to tell me his agenda for the day and I relaxed as I took in the warmth of the dancing flames.

After a short visit, I remembered what I had come over for. I took a motivational beer from the refrigerator and walked in the back room where the hillbilly car was. I took a seat next to the car, pulled the tab on my beer can, and let the car tell me the story. From the John Deer tractor seat on the front bumper to the coal oil cowl lamps and the old shot gun strapped to the back, each item on the car had a story of its own. When I sit here, look, and read all the tags with names of people who have donated their treasures, the Dolly Parton song, 'Coat of Many Colors' sticks in my mind. A single trinket donated from each person, put all together to form a new Ernie Adams masterpiece.

Ernie relaxes in his big office chair. The old, black-iron stove melts the chill off a cold afternoon and his faithful dog, Checkers, sits at his feet. Ernie proofreads some early pages of my book I had just typed that day.

After being inspired by the two full-sized hillbilly cars at the show that day, Ernie drove home in deep thought. " I went home and thought about it all afternoon," he said. "I knew in my mind what I wanted but I just wasn't sure how I was going to execute my idea."

Initially, Ernie thought about taking his first car built from refrigerators (Grandpa Dwarf) and making it into a hillbilly car. "I decided against that idea. I didn't want to tear up a car to make another," he said. "So I walked through my scrap piles to see what I had to work with." There, he found he already had most of the materials he'd need to build a new car from scratch.

He started by pulling a 2-cylinder Onan motor from a 3-wheeled mail cart. Then, using not-so-conventional materials, he began to construct the car body of a Dwarf 1929 Ford Model A. "I used everything from soup to nuts," he said. Rarely buying anything new, he always prefers to use what is available in his own backyard. For the front fenders he used the sides of an old refrigerator. The fuel tank and firewall were built from a home refrigeration casing. Two 4' florescent lights were used for the running boards. "I even handmade the spoke wheels using a Toyota bolt pattern." And from a VW door skin, he hammered out a radiator shell.

The half-pint Model A began to take shape almost overnight. Ernie made the doors and windows fully operational. The car had two headlights but only one worked; a bird's nest laid inside the other. When the chassis and body were finished, he rolled the car outside and put a garden hose to the bare steel. Within a week, a beautiful light coat of rust covered the car. Ernie said, "I already had some stuff to put on the car and then people began to donate things they wanted to see on the car." You can find a dinosaur egg hatching in the front seat and a working miniature potbelly wood stove in the rear. In the back seat, next to the stove, sits a basket with a chicken and a pig. Fastened to the rear of the car is an old shotgun and a real moonshine still donated by Duane and Vanessa Hays. Ernie attaches an aluminum tag with the person's name to all items donated.

As you walk around the car, you can read several one-liner jokes along with antique pins and buttons of all kinds.

Ernie used a Cushman 2-speed rear end with a ring and pinion so he has two speeds good for parades or car shows. There's a saying, "You should make somebody laugh every day." Ernie says, "When I show this car, I see people smile."

A few years after building the Dwarf hillbilly car, Ernie came across a 1932 American Austin motor.

He removed the Onan motor and replaced it with this 4-cylinder, 13-hp water-cooled motor. Oddly enough, this little engine resembles the Model A motor with the exhaust manifold and the updraft carburetor. It measures only 11" long with a 2" bore. A perfect fit for Ernie's hillbilly car.

Chapter 8

Crazy About
A What?

ERNIE TURNED INTO THE PARKING LOT and slowly cruised

down a short drive into a sea of classic cars. I had my camera

rolling as I watched the Dwarf '49 Mercury move forward. The sun

was setting and the twilight beams danced across the beautiful

turquoise paint. The headlamps shined ahead with a soft glow

and a gentle rumble rolled out from the straight pipes.

The little car grew closer and heads began to turn as Ernie approached a wall of spectators. Ernie turned his car into the mob and, like Moses parted the Red Sea, the crowd split and then closed in behind him. There were no open parking spaces left, so he drove a short distance into the isle and stopped. The mass formed in a circle around him as he parked his Dwarf Mercury right there in the isle. I quickly pushed the record button on my video camera. Trying hard to hold steady, I paned across the onlookers, capturing their inquisitive reactions on film. Cameras were flashing and the rumbling voices grew louder. Everyone watched patiently as Ernie opened his door, stepped out of the car, and stood up. People gasped in amazement to see Ernie's 6'-tall, lanky body rise up and tower over the pint-sized wonder. Simultaneously, the crowd closed in and surrounded the car. I continued filming and moved in closer. "Oh, my God," I heard a lady say. "Absolutely beautiful," a man commented as he held his wife's hand, leading her closer to the car.

This was the debut of Ernie's Dwarf '49 Mercury at the Scottsdale Pavilions on the weekend of the Barrett-Jackson car auction. Ernie is well known at this particular cruise night but tonight, he surprised and wowed the crowd once again. Once more in his words, he's "the new kid on the block."

When you think about the old Fords and Mercurys from 1949 to the early 50s, you know them as very large cars; big and dominate … often known as lead sleds or fat-fendered. Ernie loved the larger-than-life presence of these cars, but one year and model stood out hood over wheels as his favorite: the '49 Mercury.

In my interviews with him I had to ask why he liked the '49 Mercury. "The '49 had always been a favorite of mine," Ernie told me. He went on with his admiration toward the model for its eye-catching grille, three-piece rear window, and beautiful dash that brought class to the car. "The car was much more striking than the '50 and '51 models," he said.

James Dean made the '49 Mercury famous in the classic movie, 'Rebel Without a Cause.' In the movie, James played a troubled teenager who drove a beautiful '49 Mercury. "The '49 has been popular ever since," said Ernie. He went on to say, "All the guys I ran with back then related the '49 Mercury with James Dean."

The crowd waits for Ernie to step out at the Scottsdale Pavilions

Ernie poses for pictures

A picture is worth a thousand words.
When seeing is not believing, sometimes Ernie has to show photos
of how he built his Dwarf cruiser. Even after seeing photos, some
walk away shaking their heads.

Photo by Lyle Aguilera

Ernie pauses momentarily for a picture while
working on his Dwarf '49 Mercury.

It seemed as if it was only yesterday when my father shared his idea of building a scaled-down Mercury. I've been fortunate to be around the shop and watch him build his dreams. I was there day to day and observed the Dwarf Mercury take shape. Piece by piece, I saw the car go from an idea to reality. One thing though, I did not know the beginning of the story. I had to search threw countless video interviews I had done with my father until I found the story I was searching for.

Ernie began construction on his new Dwarf in September 2004. "When I decided that my next car would be a Dwarf '49 Mercury, the first thing I had to do was find a Toyota donor car." Not sure where to look, he said, "I just kept my ears and eyes open." He continued with the story of him driving in Phoenix one day and came upon a train stopped on the tracks. He waited a minute then turned down a side street with hopes of going around the train at the next block.

Half way down the block, from the corner of his eye he caught a glimpse of a front fender, headlight and part of a grille. HE stepped on the brake and pulled to the curbside. With a smile, he said, "I knew that fender and headlight as soon as I saw them." Ernie got out and walked up to an old, red-brick house with a fenced yard to the west. Sure enough, covered halfway with an old piece of carpet and a bougainvillea vine, there sat a 1976 Toyota Corolla. "That's the car I'd been looking for," said Ernie. He walked to the front and gave a knock. The door opened and there stood a little, old man. "Hello," said Ernie. "I was driving by and noticed your old Toyota in the yard," he told the man. The man looked up at Ernie and said, "That car's no good. It hasn't run in 20 years." Ernie told the man, "I'd be interested in buying it if it was for sale." "Come and get it out of my yard and you can have it," the man replied. "Yes sir, I'll come this afternoon and pick it up," Ernie graciously offered.

When Ernie got his donor car home, he unloaded it out back behind his shop and started right in. The first thing he did was unbolt everything that would unbolt off the car: springs, doors, engine, transmission. "Everything that would unbolt, I took," said Ernie. Next, he took the torch and cut out the spare tire carrier along with the firewall and part of the floorpan. The engine, transmission, driveshaft and rear end were set aside for the drivetrain. He built a homemade straight axle for the front, then he used the Toyota spindles. This allowed the Toyota wheel pattern to match and the disc brakes can also be used. "I can use the brake lines, all the electrical, and rear springs to," explained Ernie. He adds,

"I have to recoil the springs to the length I need. I asked what he does with all the other parts left over, and Ernie replied, "I don't use them but I take them all out of the car anyway and store them in an old fifth-wheel trailer I use as my spare parts house." The doors were striped for the window mechanism and the indoor latches. The steering column and sector would also be put to use.

When Ernie starts to build a Dwarf, he brings a homemade channel iron frame jig in the shop and stations it where he's going to build his car.

As I look over my recorded interviews of Ernie, I can see him look off to the side, then to the ceiling. I watch as he takes off his glasses and rubs his forehead. It's been a few years since all this was done and he has to think back in his mind to recall the events I'm inquiring about. Often before an interview, I'll give him a picture or two and have him study them for a moment. Once I get him to the place and time I'm asking about, the information flows right out.

Ernie cut 8" from the rear end and set it in place on the frame jig. The front axle is built to match the width of the rear axle and also set in place. Now, Ernie positions the engine where he needs it and adds the frame rails. When asked what's next, Ernie replies, "Now I refer back to a picture of the car that I'm using to build off and go on with building the side rails to the frame."

DWARF 1949 MERCURY

The Dwarf car has been created and revolutionized by Ernie Adams. From the backyard, to the racetrack, and then onto the street. One man's dream of building a small, homemade car that he could ride in. If he only knew when he built that first car out of old refrigerators, where it would take him … Ernie said to me, "When I was little, I wished I would never grow up so I could ride in my little cars." Ernie did grow up and he's still riding in his little cars.

Saturday morning May 19: Running behind, I choke down a cup of coffee and hurry out the door. I spin my truck wheels in the dirt drive and set into an easy drift out the gate. Driving just above the speed limit, I was on my way to my brother Rick's house, two miles down the road. There's a car show today in Miami, Arizona and I'm catching a ride with him. The plan is to meet Ernie and three other cars in a parking lot in Maricopa. We roll into town right on time. I could see Ernie in his Dwarf '49 Mercury alongside of Gene Tweedy in his '54 Chevy Bel Air. A fellow named John in a T-Bucket pulls in behind Rick and I. No sooner did we open the car doors and Ted drives up in his '52 Chevy convertible. I heard Ernie shout out, "Let's go!" We all followed behind the Dwarf and were on our way.

Ernie led the pack in his little Mercury. Testing the speed limit, we rolled along at 70 to 75 mph. Rick and I followed up the rear. John and his T-Bucket were in front of us, when we heard a loud 'BOOM!' Smoke bellowed out of the T-Bucket and oil inundated the highway. A piece of steel bounced out from under the car and stuck fast in a roadside bush. The T-Bucket quickly pulled to

the side and John got out. He took his hat off and scratches his head. Rick and I swung in behind him and stepped out of the car. After looking the car over, John noticed the governor cover on the transmission had blown off. "That's what I saw fly out the bottom. It's in a bush a few hundred feet back," I said. Using a rock as a makeshift hammer, John smacked the cover into place, added ATF fluid, and we were once again on our way.

At the show, we all sat in a half-circle behind Ernie's little Mercury and bullshit as the spectators eagerly looked over the car. One guy said, "I'd feel like a big man if I had this car." Another said, "I could fit in there." "Climb in. You'd be surprised," said Ernie. A tall man with a cowboy hat and beer belly said to Ernie, "You should build a '57 Chevy." Ernie replied with a smile, "I think a '55 Ford would be a much prettier car." The tall cowboy looked closer at the car, running his hands across the fenders and onto the front bumper. "How do you shape the parts," he asked? Ernie answers, "With a torch in one hand and a hammer in the other."

Ernie parks his Dwarf Mercury alongside of a 1940 Buick. Here you can clearly distinguish the difference between a full-sized automobile and a Ernie Adams Dwarf cruiser.

chapter 9

Dwarf Mercury On The Mother Road

ROUNDING THE LAST WIDE BEND into Seligman, Arizona, the first thing I see is an old, abandoned gas station. The pumps were still attached and an old pop machine was left standing outside the front-office door. Like many others, the station is from a time gone past. Quietly resting there, now only a part of the memories of America's most famous highway, ROUTE 66.

Like a page from time, Ernie's Dwarf sits beside the old gas pumps.

Ernie's been going on the Arizona Route 66 Fun Run for 16 years now. A 140-mile excursion from Seligman to Topock/Golden Shores, Arizona. A traveling car show along the old Route 66 Highway, through 11 towns pushed aside and almost forgotten after the completion of the I-40 in 1984. This year is the long-awaited debut of Ernie's Dwarf '49 Mercury.

Our Journey begins at the Waffle House on Bell Road in north Phoenix. As I rolled into the parking lot, I could see the little Mercury right away. Not hard to spot with six guys standing around the car wondering what they're looking at. Next to Ernie's Dwarf Mercury was Gene Tweedy's 1954 Chevy Bel Air and Billy Schwing's 1957 Ford with the Y-block motor. Both Gene and Billy are making the run with Ernie this year. After a short, three-car show in the parking lot, we made our way inside for a bite to eat. I walked in ahead and took a booth by myself so I could do some filming of the guys. Ernie walked through the door first. "Hello Ernie," said the waitress as if she had just seen him yesterday. "You got a new little car this year?" she asked. Ernie smiled and said, "Yep, can we get three coffees?" After a two-egg special breakfast our Route 66 journey began.

**We Stayed Here at the ASH FORK INN,
Ash Fork, Arizona on Route 66**

We got on the I-17, northbound toward Flagstaff. Our first stop was Cordes Junction to meet up with old Mac, a friend of Ernie's.

Ernie pulls into the Chevron station with Gene and Billy behind. Mac was standing outside the station in tattered jeans and a dirty shirt, excited to see Ernie's new Dwarf. Ernie climbs out of his little car and Mac greets him with a handshake. No sooner did we say hello and we were saying goodbye. In our cars and headed to Prescott Valley, then onto Ash Fork, where we had our rooms reserved for the night.

When we approached the main drag of Ash Fork, the old buildings looked quiet and lifeless. I saw an old DeSoto car sitting up on top of a building. The sign said DeSoto's Salon. The streets were empty as we drove past a few old motels and on through town. We made good time driving and arrived early. Just as we were almost out of town, we came upon our rustic, old motel. Not a fancy place, I'd say. The tall, old sign said ASH FORK INN $29. At first appearance, I wondered if it was even open.

After settling in our rooms for a short rest, there was an abrupt knock at the door. "Let go," said Ernie. And just like that, we were off again.

As we drove into Seligman, I followed Ernie on through town until we came to the Black Cat Bar. Ernie pulled up and parked in front, along the sidewalk. A man walked right over and told Ernie, "Pull up next to my Buick so I can get a picture." Another guy said, "My wife wants to know if you could make her an Oldsmobile?" Ernie just gave him a grin.

We made the once up and around the town then ended up at The Road Kill Café. Certainly, an appetizing-sounding name for a café, we went inside for lunch. When our waitress came around, Ernie ordered up two dead skunks.

The lady patiently let him know that they were fresh out of skunk and offered up a burger instead.

As we ate our lunch, through the window we watch the little, old-west town begin to come alive. Throughout the afternoon, the town continued to fill up. The motel parking lots overflowed with cool old cars and people mingled throughout looking at one another's rides. I walked along the sidewalk with my video and still camera, people-watching and imagining back to the days when these old cars owned the roads.

I remembered my dad telling me about The Snow Cap Drive-In and what a cool place it was. I had to go see this for myself. As I walked closer, I could hear some good oldies music playing and there were a few people dancing around in the street. A guy with a guitar and a lady with a large afro wig were putting on a little show for all the cars cruising by. I watched for a moment, quite entertained when I saw Ernie's little Mercury cruise right up in front of the Snow Cap and park. The lady with the big hair said, "That's Ernie." She walked right over and proceeded to play the hood of Ernie's car like a piano. People immediately began to gather around and watch the sideshow. Next, the big-haired lady stooped over and poked her head inside the passenger window. "Hi Ernie," she said. "I just love it," she squealed. Ernie's reply was, "Open the door and climb in." Wasting no time, she pulled open the door and sat her butt down in the seat, pausing shortly for a picture. Then Ernie said, "I've got to go." With that, he turned the key, revved the pipes, and off he went.

When Ernie left, I took a closer look around the Snow Cap. I could see some old cars around back so I walked that way. Just like a scene from the Disney movie Cars, there were several old cars with eyeballs in the front windows and some nice, old gas pumps standing along the side.

Right: **Ernie and his Dwarf 1949 Mercury**
at THE SNOW CAP DRIVE-IN, Seligman, Arizona

Ernie filled his tank Saturday morning in Seligman, Arizona. People gathered around for a one-car show.

Later that evening, we found ourselves back at The Road Kill Café for dinner. As we were walking in, here comes Billy with his '57 Ford, just in time to join us. Billy is a comical old boy from Oklahoma. After a story he told us about a union job initiation involving a goat, I watched Ernie wipe the tears from his eyes from laughing so hard.

The next morning was Saturday. We made the 22-mile trip from our motel in Ash Fork back to Seligman for the start of the Route 66 Fun Run. Route 66 is actually the main road that runs through Seligman. What a site to see, as we cruised in through town. A line of old cars as far as you could see, all lined up for the Fun Run start. We drove right passed them all and into the café parking lot for breakfast. I asked my dad, "Shouldn't we get in line with the other cars?"

"I like to take my time and leave when I'm ready," he replies. "All those cars line up and head out at the same time, then clog up all along the way," he added.

The sidewalks were full of people walking and gazing at all the beautiful cars. We watched through the café window as people snapped picture after picture of Ernie's little Mercury. "There have been more pictures taken of my car than George Barris ever had," said Ernie.

The excitement of the Route 66 Fun Run was building. We finished our breakfast and headed to the parking lot where a small crowed was still standing around Ernie's car. It was 10:00 when the first assemblages of cars were turned loose. Unlike the way they trickled into town, they headed out like a title wave.

Ernie was of the last bunch of cars to leave. He said, "I'm not going to hurry, just to sit in a traffic jam." I went on ahead so I could film his car at various stages of the run.

***Ernie and Gene Tweedy pull in for gas
at an old station in Truxton, Arizona.***

The first town we came to after Seligman was Grand Canyon Caverns. We drove right on through and headed for Peach Springs. I pulled off in Peach Springs and set up my cameras at the bottom of a long, winding curve as you come into town. It was just a few minutes before I could hear the crackle of Ernie's strait pipes as he rounded the bend. Gene was close behind, leading a string of Model-As.

The first town we stopped in was Truxton. There were people lined along the highway in lawn chairs as we drove through town. Ernie pulled into an old-time gas station and up to the pumps. The bell rang ding, ding as each tire ran over an air hose. Gene pulled up to the old pumps next to Ernie. Ding, ding goes the bell and the gas attendant appears for full-service pumping. I'm thinking what a great picture this is. I set up my video camera and snapped some awesome shots before a small crowd gathered for the same opportunity.

After our brief stop in Truxton we were on our way again, headed for Valentine. We had no plans to stop in Valentine; we just drove right through, waving at the onlookers as we passed by.

The town of Hackberry was next on our itinerary. Again, I hurried ahead of Ernie so I could film him as he pulled into town. I was caught by surprise when I rounded the last bend into town. Cars lined both sides of the highway a quarter of a mile before I even got into town. A guide was directing cars into an old gas station. By luck, I found a small spot where I could park on the highway.

I had my cameras ready when Ernie arrived. He pulled in right past the parking guide and stopped in front of the old gas pumps. This was the busiest place yet on our journey. Ernie got everyone's attention when he pulled up. He turned the car off, climbed out, and stood up tall beside his Dwarf mercury. People looked in amazement to seen such a tall man get out of such a diminutive car. Ernie waited there for a moment while the crowd snapped several pictures.

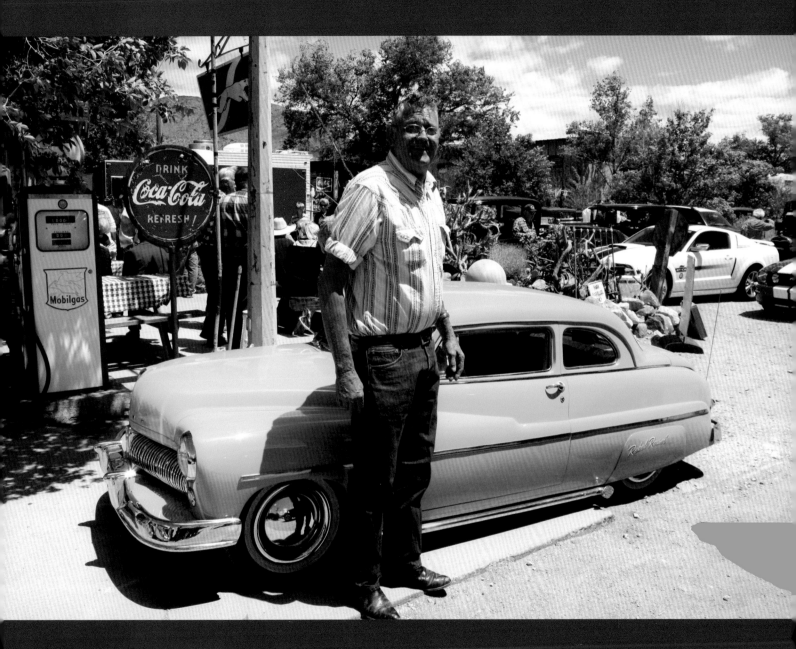

Ernie poses for pictures next to his Dwarf 1949 Mercury in Hackberry, Arizona.

The Hackberry station was a playground for nostalgia enthusiast. Old gas station signs filled the walls. Rusted cars and old farm machines were scattered throughout the parking area. A Model-A parts graveyard rested upon a small hill overlooking the station.

Ernie stands in front of a cool, old garage in Hackberry, Arizona.

"You have to check out the men's room," said Ernie with a suspicious look on his face. When I found my way there, I had to wait for two others in front of me. My turn now … I walked in and closed the door. Wow! I thought to myself. How could anyone do their business with wall-to-wall half-naked women watching you? Every inch of the restroom walls was filled with pictures of very sexy ladies.

Ernie, Gene and I made our way around the side of the station where we could listen to a band playing golden oldies. Ernie said to me, "Look at that old garage." To our right was a depiction of how an old farm garage would have looked in the 1940s or '50s. Several flathead V-8 motors, Model-A wheels, and a very nice Model-T truck were among the garage decor.

We stood there gawking for a few minutes, then Ernie said, "Let's go!" When Ernie decides he's ready to go, he's leaving with you or without you. We had another big car show in Kingman at 3:00. Everyone in the Fun Run will stay the night there and then get back on Route 66 in the morning.

When we got into Kingman, we followed the old highway through town until we came to a huge Route 66 sign downtown. To enter the show, you had to drive right through the big highway sign. As far as I could see down the street, there were cars backed in along both sides. Ernie found an open spot beside a black El Camino and promptly seized the opportunity.

We set up lawn chairs behind the little Mercury and visited with people as they walked by. Two young men walk up and asked if they could get a picture by the dwarf. Ernie told the guys, "Sure, take all the pictures you want." The two walk around the car and stood alone the side. Then they took off their shoes, placed them on the ground, and kneeled down with their knees inside their shoes. They looked like a couple of dwarfs next to the Dwarf car. As people walked by, many would say hello to Ernie as if they were good friends. "So many people seem to know who I am," he said. "I can't remember all of them," he added.

The next morning was Sunday, the last day of our trip. We kicked things off at the Powerhouse Museum. When we arrived, the lot was full of cars. Right away, we spotted Billy Shwing's '57 Ford. Ernie pulled in next to Billy and Gene and parked on the next row. Right away, a small crowd gathered to see Ernie's new Dwarf. Inside the Powerhouse, they were hosting a pancake breakfast and a good band played while we ate. When we finished the last of our coffee, Ernie looked at me and said, "You ready to go?" From here, were headed to Cool Springs and onto the old western town of Oatman.

Ernie visits with some old friends at the Powerhouse Visitor Center in Kingman, Arizona.

Twenty-three miles from Kingman to Oatman. They were 23 miles of some of the most beautiful landscape I've ever seen. Old Route 66 became very narrow as it wound tightly through rugged mountains. I found it hard to imagine how people made their way across the rough desert in such primitive times. I was following behind my dad and, without warning, he steered off the road onto a narrow shoulder. Ernie put his hand out and motioned me to pull up next to him. "Go on ahead," he said. You can film us as we come up the hill at Sitgreaves Pass. I wasted no time moving on up the road. Along my way through the hills, I came upon Cool Springs. All I saw here was a really cool old-time gas station with a full parking lot. A man stood out front holding a sign reading, 'Old Cars Only.' I slowed down to get a good look, then continued on. I wound my way up the steep, narrow old highway until I found a pull-off on the roadside. I grabbed my cameras and stepped out of the car. Looking down over the edge of the long, curvy mountain road I could see Ernie's little Dwarf Mercury as it rounded the tight bends. Gene and a whole string of classic cruisers followed right behind. I was able to set my video camera on the trunk lid and film as I simultaneously snapped some really nice still shots of Ernie and the group passing by.

Then back in my car and up the hill I went. When I reached the top of Sitgreaves Pass, I could see Ernie already making his way down the other side. The loud crackle of straight pipes echoed through the tall mountain walls. The low gears were doing their best to slow the little Mercury. "Sounded like you were popping corn," said Gene later at lunch.

When we reached Oatman, traffic came to a halt just inside the town. I could see three cars ahead of me, and a donkey was standing in the middle of the road. Not concerned about moving, he stood there and looked at us momentarily before gradually loping off to the side. Oatman is a picturesque town right out of an old western movie, complete with live animals roaming the street and gun-fighting cowboys. I walked with Ernie and Gene along the old storefronts. The sidewalks were wooden planks laid in a row, just as you'd expect an old western town to have. Ernie stopped in front of a door and opened it to peek inside. "Let's go in here," he said. A sign hung in front that read 'Oatman Hotel, Restaurant & Bar 1902.' Gene and I followed Ernie and stepped inside. At first glance, I was taken by surprise. I'd never seen wallpaper like this before. From top to bottom, the walls were covered in dollar bills throughout the whole restaurant.

After buffalo burgers and a cold beer, we tipped the waitress and stepped outside. There in the street was a cowboy pulling a little, red covered wagon. As he stomped down the street there were bangs and crashing sounds. Little bells chimed as he strummed a washboard attached to his chest. All these sounds in rhythm made him sort of a one-man band and quite an entertaining site.

The cars began to flow out of Oatman. "Time to go," said Ernie and we headed down the road. Now, on the last leg of our journey, we head for Topock/ Golden Shores.

At the finish line, Ernie drove his Dwarf Mercury through a giant Route 66 sign and posed for a picture. "Pull over here so I can get a picture of your car next to mine," said Ernie's friend, Mud. People gathered around and watched the two Mercurys of very different proportions line up side by side for photos. After a few pictures with cars, we were ready to head for home. Ernie said to me, "That's what the Route 66 Fun Run is all about for me, meeting people, taking pictures, and traveling with people that like to drive their cars." He ends with, "I have a lot of fun with my car and people can see what it's all about when they travel with me."

*Right: **Ernie crossing the Route 66 Fun Run finish line in Topock/Golden Shores.***

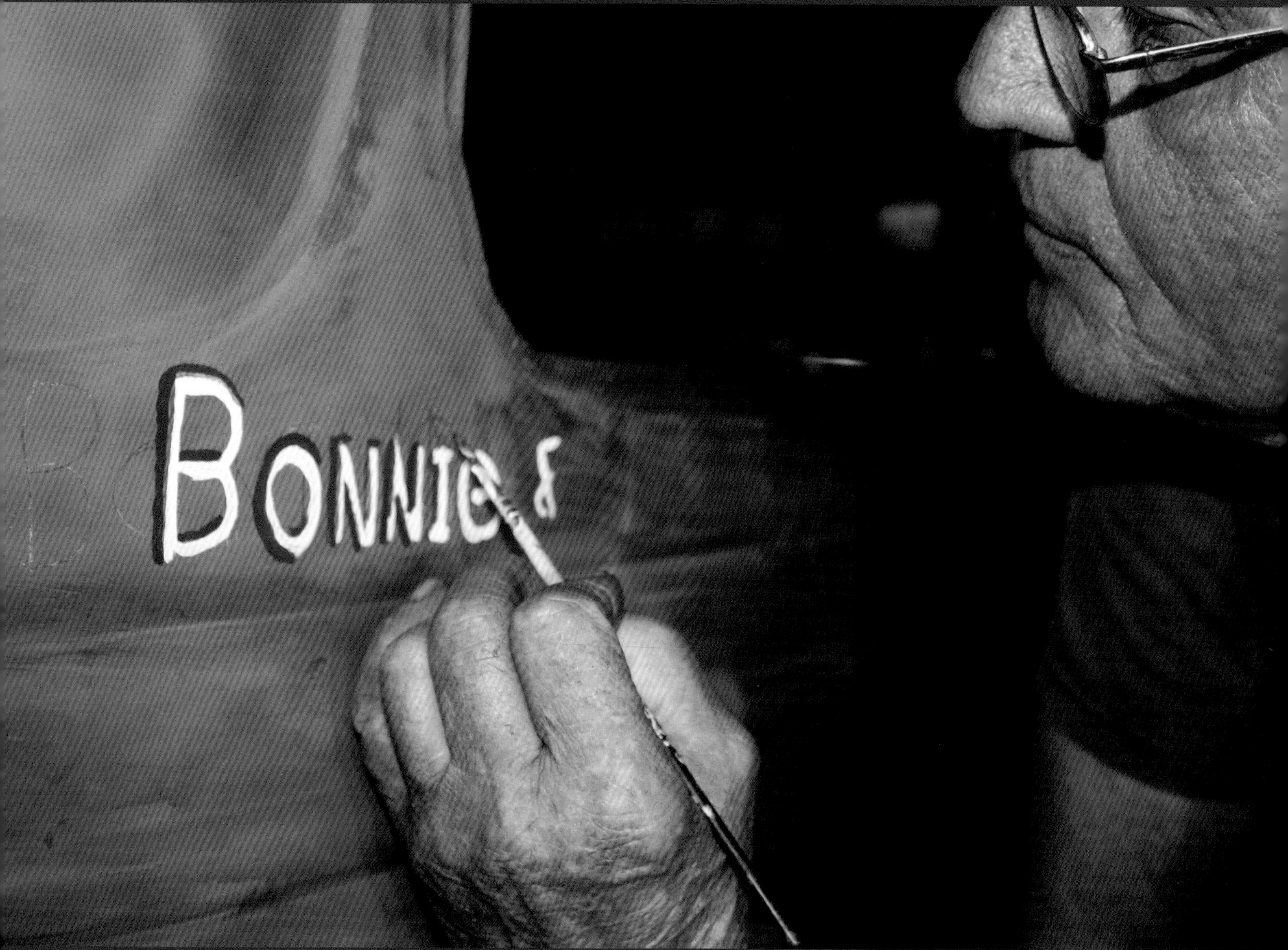
BONNIE &

Chapter 10

Bonnie

"I MET A MAN IN LINCOLN, NEBRASKA at the Americruise car show. He had a 1934 Ford 2-door sedan." "It was total rust, with a nice motor, and it just looked good that way," said Ernie. He stopped the man and said to him, "I hope you don't finish this car." The man gave a smile and replied, "It is finished." Ernie added, "The car was beautiful that way."

The 1934 Ford 2-door sedan. "One of the most beautiful bodies of any car," said Ernie. He boasted, "I call this my Rat Rod. I just left it all natural with the bare steel and a light coat of rust." Although the body appears natural and rustic, the beautiful chrome shines out to highlight all the handsome features of the car. Ernie has always been fond of '34 Fords. "I like the look of the suicide doors and the overall shape of the louvered pattern in the hood," he notes. One chrome horn rests upon each fender like jewelry along the sides of a long, slanted grille. The hood ornament is a 1935 Auburn flying lady. The rusted spoke wheels match the overall looks of the body more than any fancy wheels would.

"When I decided to build this car, I had to start with the spoke wheels," said Ernie. "I knew the only way I was going to get authentic 1934 Ford spoke wheels was to make them myself."

Right: **All the beautiful handmade chrome brings the bare steel body to life.**

With a hammer in one hand and a torch in the other, Ernie shaped
the centerpiece he'll use for the '34 Ford spoke wheels.

Ernie is a modern-day blacksmith. He's a master at heating a flat piece of steel and shaping it into something you're sure came right from the factory.

With a steady hand, Ernie works the spokes into place.

From a Toyota 13"-wheel, Ernie cuts out the center, leaving only the out-side band. Next, he built a homemade jig to hold the band and assemble the wheel. A total of 32 spokes were cut to length and woven through the outer band and into the handmade center piece that incorporates the Toyota wheel bolt pattern. A total of five wheels were made, one being a spare that mounts above the rear bumper.

He used the Toyota rear end and cut a total of 10-¾" out, an equal amount on each side. The new spoke wheels were then bolted to the rear end without the tires. For the front, he built a handmade straight axle and used ball joints instead of the king pins. "I used the Toyota spindles so I could utilize the Toyota disc brakes," said Ernie.

Then he attached the front spoke wheels to the straight axle. On a large steel frame, he set front and rear axles in place. The overall layout of the car was now set up. The frame and body were ready to be built.

Ernie spot-welds the body panel on his Dwarf '34 Ford.

Friday afternoon, I left my house early for break time at Ernie's. I tried to sneak in and catch him working in a natural state whenever possible. I quietly pulled in front of the big, steel shop, got out, and clicked my door closed. I could hear the familiar buzz of Ernie's welder. I walked in through the large sliding doors with my camera in hand, ready for anything. For a minute or two, I snapped pictures and shot a bit of video until unsuspecting Ernie raised his welding hood to see me standing there. "Time for a beer?" he asked. I say no and briefly explained my intensions. Go on back to work so I can get more footage of you building your car.

Minutes later, I could hear the sound of quads and a sand rail. The neighbors, Daren and Marie, arrived first and Raymond in his dune buggy right behind them. Roger and my brother, Rick, arrived next along with my mom, who walked in the door right behind them. A sure sign it's break time at Ernie's again.

Ernie holds the steering wheel frame next to the beer box mold.

Most every piece on Ernie's cars had to be hand-made from scratch. Even the steering wheel is no exception. Using 7/16" cold-roll steel, he shaped the wheel and added three spokes like the original 1934 Ford steering wheel. Then, the horn button is made using the centerpiece spline from the Toyota so that it looked just like the real one. "I put the steel framing part of the steering wheel down inside a cardboard mold I made from a beer box." "Then I fill it with boat resin," said Ernie. "When I removed the wheel from the beer box mold, I used an electric grinder to cut all the finger notches," he added. Ernie hand-sanded the wheel to get the final finish, then reassembled the horn button.

Left: **I've been privileged to capture each step of Ernie building his Dwarf 1934 Ford sedan.**

As I walk around Ernie's shop among all the Dwarf cars I can only say again how much of a "wonderment" this continues to be in my mind. The "how did he do that" will never cease. To be here in person makes it all reality. Plus, there are 2 cars being built. WOW

Enjoy the update

Lloyd

Lloyd Willey

You must have an elaborate shop to build cars like that, people would often say to Ernie. He usually would look to the ground, shake his head slowly, and with a smile simply say, "Nope, just the basics." Many times, I walked in the shop and Ernie would show me a piece of steel. He'd say something like, "This is going to be my headlight rings," or "This will be my door handle." I watch him put a piece of steel in a vice, strike the torch and hammer it into what you would believe is a factory part.

Being naturally ambidextrous, Ernie can weld equally as good with his left hand as he can with his right. This extraordinary talent, the accurate eye, and the steady regimented hands are obvious in his car building. In Ernie's work, it is easy to see his precise craftsmanship and deep imagination. He makes the impossible look easy. To see Ernie's cars in person leaves little doubt that their creator has remarkable talent.

Ernie does some last-minute preparation before attempting to start his Dwarf '34 Ford for the first time.

It was a frigid-cold evening in January. Like a mirage in the desert sand, I could see a dim light shine through the faded-green fiber panels that lined the top of Ernie's tall building. I was on my way home late in the evening, around 9:00. My old truck heater was working hard to put out any warm air. I knew my dad would have the wood stove roaring-hot. I convinced myself, I'd stop for one beer and see what's up. As I pulled up, I could smell the scent of burning pine drifting through the cold breeze. I opened the door and walked inside. The old wood stove roared as the hot-steel chimney sucked the air threw the half-opened doors on the stove. Startled a bit and surprised to see a visitor at this time of night, Ernie excitedly said, "Hey your just in time … I'm going to start my car for the first time."

Loose wires draped across the engine and the fuel line dangled inside a glass peanut butter jar half filled with fuel. Ernie said, "Do you have your video camera?" "Yes, in my car," I replied. I slipped outside and grabbed my cameras. The lighting was perfect. I steadied my camera on the passenger door and filmed Ernie's hands as he turned the ignition key. I heard a soft click. Next, he pushed in the starter button as I held my breath in anticipation. The engine cranked one, two, three times then, with a pop and a bang, came to life. Ernie

**Ernie turns the key for the first time and
starts the Dwarf 1934 Ford.**

listened close as he dialed it in. The two straight pipes that stretched out the
back began to sing a song we loved to hear. Ernie turned the key off and said,
"I think those pipes are going to work great." "I can't run it long without water,"
he commented. "I just wanted to hear it run."

Ernie's Old Mill wood-burning stove

It was a chilly January evening, just after dinner. I took a seat next to Ernie's hillbilly Dwarf and sank into deep thought on some photography I needed. Suddenly, I looked up to see Ernie with his eyes wide open as if he'd seen a ghost. "The stove is floating," he said talking at the top of his breath. I hurried behind him. "Get your camera," he said. "The stove is floating." I knew my dad liked beer but he's drinking coffee. I'm thinking, what's going on? I followed him around the corner to the stove. What I was seeing I did not believe. Just as Ernie had said, the heavy iron stove was hovering above the concrete floor, slowly swaying side to side. We both gazed in amazement. I would guess the stove to weigh about 250 pounds, but there it was seemingly weightless. Reality soon sat in and we knew there had to be a logical explanation for this phenomenon. Attached to the rear of the stove was a heavy, black-iron chimney pipe. The pipe became so hot that it began to flex, lifting the stove right off the ground. Knowing others would scoff at the floating stove, Ernie said, "Turn on your camera and film this." I filmed and Ernie narrated, "You can see this stove is floating above the floor. When I die, I'll come back and haunt people by lifting this stove."

Chapter 11

"I Just Want to Build My Cars"

PICTURE THIS IF YOU CAN. I'm 6' tall and 210 lbs. Ernie is six feet tall as well. The two of us are about to get in a car that's only 48" tall and 50" wide. Ernie got in first, with ease. It's my turn now. I opened the passenger door and paused a moment while I assessed the best way to climb inside. First, I swung my left leg in and sat down. Next, I pulled my right leg in and closed the door—all in one swift motion. Wow, no problem at all. Here we are, two grown men in a pint-sized Chevy that's surprisingly roomy and comfortable.

For 23 years now, Ernie's been building his Dwarf cruisers. I must confess that I have yet to ride in one. One bright Saturday afternoon. I let my dad in on this. I could see a look of surprise on his face. "Could you give me a ride?" I asked him. "OK," said Ernie and off he went to get his little '39 Chevy.

Ernie turned the key and the engine fired on cue. The mighty little Toyota motor roared like a V-8 with the long duel straight pipes. Immediately, I was grinning from ear to ear. Out goes the clutch and off we go. I can't believe I haven't done this long before now. Down the long, dirt drive we went and out onto the paved street. Still amazed and wearing a great, big grin; Ernie quickly shifted up through a few gears. I watched the speedometer climb higher … 50, 60 and then 70 mph. The straight exhaust pipes sang a song as we glided down the road. WOW, I'm saying to myself, this is everything I imagined and so much more. This car rides better than the real thing. As we drove along, we passed by a few cars on the road. I could see passengers' heads turn with expressions of, 'what in the world is that'?

Back into the long, dirt drive and up into the shop we went. The car rolled to a stop and Ernie turned the key to the off position. Getting out was just as easy as climbing in. I closed the solid door with a tight click. Still smiling, I said, "Thank you."

Left: **After 23 years, I finally got my first ride in a Dwarf cruiser**

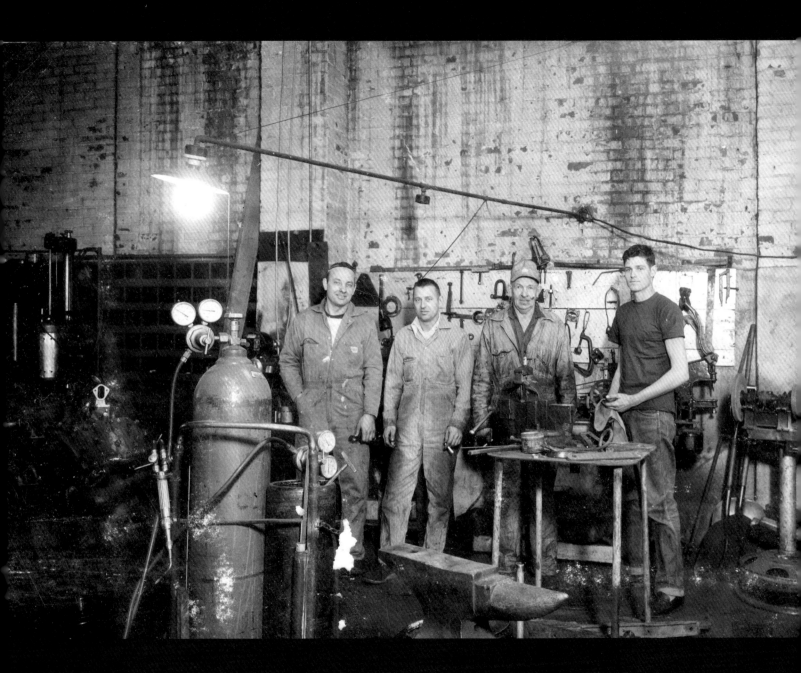

Ernie's first job was at Frank & Jacks garage in Harvard, Nebraska.

Top Right: **Ernie builds the grille for his Dwarf '34 Ford using a 1½" pipe.**

Bottom Right: **Ernie proudly stands by his finished product.**

Ernie and his fat cat, Pokey

Today, I have off from work. It's a nice warm day, too nice to work inside on my computer. I decided to wonder over to see what my dad is doing today and maybe have a cold beer with him. When I walked inside the shop, he was sitting in his big office chair with his fat cat Pokey stretched across his lap. Merle Haggard was playing on the 8-track stereo. I took a chair, opened my beer, and we began to talk. Most often, the conversation will follow the subject of cars. Ernie has a photographic memory when it comes to car body styles, year and makes. He can recite details from front bumpers to rear tail fins for most any old car. Today, we got on the subject of stainless strips on old Chevrolets. "1942 to 1948 Chevys have a series of stainless strips along the front and rear fenders," he said. On a small piece of paper, he drew me a crude picture. Then he turned his chair to the side, leaned over, and pulled out a big book about Chevrolets

Ernie draws a crude picture of stainless strips on a 1942 Chevrolet then shows me them in a book.

from the shelf next to him. "Look here," he said as he thumbed through pages of body styles. I stood up and took a closer seat next to him. When he located the page he was searching for, he stopped and pointed his grease-stained index finger to a '42 model. Sure enough, there were the Chevrolet body styles for the 1942 and the stainless strips just as he showed me in his rough drawing on the scratch paper.

From the 1942 Chevy we went to the '43, '44 and up through 1948.

When we had gone through all the Chevrolets, Ernie got up and disappeared around the corner. I rolled my chair back a few feet and took another cold beer from the refrigerator. Seconds later, Ernie reappeared with a book on old Fords. Fantastic! I couldn't think of a better way to spend a quiet afternoon.

As we went from car to car in that book on old Fords, each one would trigger memories. Ernie would tell me short stories about someone who had that particular car or a time when he rode in one. I patiently listened through every story, thinking how lucky I am to share these special times with my dad.

Ernie builds the fenders for his Dwarf 1940 Mercury coupe.

Because of their different lengths, Ernie has to make each grille bar individually.

Break Time at Ernie's

It's Friday afternoon on a brisk January day. I had just put the last tool in its place and closed the tool chest drawer.

Today, my brother, Rick, and I prepped the shop for painting Ernie's Dwarf '49 Mercury. We hung large sheets of plastic to contain the paint and covered the other cars to protect them from over-spray. Mitch Webber, my son-in-law is going to prep and shoot the paint for Ernie's Dwarf. He's on his way over now.

Ready to have a seat and relax, I pulled over the closest chair and sat down. Rick opened the refrigerator and asked, "Ready for a beer?" He could see from the look I gave him that no answer was needed. As he handed me a beer, I heard two car doors close outside the shop and the sound of a quad in the near distance, getting closer. I opened my beer and drew a long swallow. Inside the door walked Bonnie and her daughter, Terri. "Hey Kevin," said Bonnie. Ernie looked up and asks, "Break time?" I heard the quad engine shut off and in walked Daren and Marie. Marie carried in her hand a large bag of rib bones, "Kevin, I brought your dog some bones," she said.

Daren wasted no time walking over to look at Ernie's progress on the grille bars of his Dwarf '40 Mercury. Ernie stood up, then walked over to the large, steel shop doors and pulled one shut, then the other. Next, he sashayed over to the old iron stove and knelt down to see if any hot coals remained. With the flicker of a few red coals Ernie brought some kindling to a nice, orange flame, then stocked it full of wood. Within a few minutes, I could hear the fire roar from across the round table.

Just then, the side door opened and my mom stepped inside. "Hello," she said. As the story telling for the afternoon begins, the sound of another quad rumbles up to the shop. Silence fell over the group as we listen and pondered who it could be. Almost simultaneously, we all blurt out, "Roger."

Gene Tweedy, still working on his Dwarf '54 Chevy, finished the last weld on his stainless strips. He draped the mixing chamber over the gas bottles and headed toward the refrigerator. Roger entered the shop and took a seat off to the side. "Hello," I say to Roger. Again, the sounds of car doors grab our attention. The shop door opened with a loud creek and then slammed shut, sending a shimmer throughout the building. In walked Mitch Webber, arms full of painting materials, and my daughter Heather followed behind with a 12-pack of beer.

Fifteen of us total for this afternoon's break time crowd. The stories for the day bounced around the group and the bright-orange flames danced in the old wood-burning stove. The warmth of good friends fills the shop, for it's break time at Ernie's once again.

Ernie cuts and shapes the entire car body from flat steel.

Here, the body is close to completion. The front and rear bumpers are next.

Ernie's Dwarf 1940 chopped-top Mercury 2-door coupe

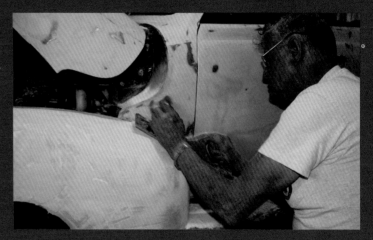

Ernie Adams, a true artist.

Ernie gets the continuous question,
"What are you going to build next?"
Ernie's typical answer is, "Oh, I don't know."

WHAT WOULD YOU GUESS?